D1360389

The Frugal Innovator

Creating Change on a Shoestring Budget

The Frugal Innovator

Charles Leadbeater

First published 2014 by
PALGRAVE MACMILLAN

Palgrave Macmillan in the UK is an imprint of Macmillan Publishers Limited,
registered in England, company number 785998, of Houndmills, Basingstoke,
Hampshire RG21 6XS.

Palgrave Macmillan in the US is a division of St Martin's Press LLC,
175 Fifth Avenue, New York, NY 10010.

Palgrave Macmillan is the global academic imprint of the above companies
and has companies and representatives throughout the world.

Palgrave® and Macmillan® are registered trademarks in the United States,
the United Kingdom, Europe and other countries.

ISBN 978–1–137–33536–4

This book is printed on paper suitable for recycling and made from fully
managed and sustained forest sources. Logging, pulping and manufacturing
processes are expected to conform to the environmental regulations of the
country of origin.

A catalogue record for this book is available from the British Library.

A catalog record for this book is available from the Library of Congress.

Typeset by MPS Limited, Chennai, India.

*For
Iris M. Bedell,
the original frugal innovator*

Contents

Acknowledgements ╱ viii
Preface: The Surfer and the Wave ╱ x

1   **Ask for the Impossible** ╱ 1

2   **The Rush** ╱ 8

3   **The Squeeze** ╱ 19

4   **The Crunch** ╱ 34

5   **The Swell** ╱ 46

6   **Lean** ╱ 58

7   **Simple** ╱ 78

8   **Clean** ╱ 96

9   **Social** ╱ 121

10   **Who, How, Where?** ╱ 140

11   **In Reverse** ╱ 159

12   **Our Frugal Future** ╱ 181

References ╱ 189
Bibliography ╱ 194
Index ╱ 196

Acknowledgements

I would like to thank all the people who have made this book possible. I have drawn on the intellectual inspiration of many sources, including C. K. Prahalad's groundbreaking work *The Fortune at the Bottom of the Pyramid* and the pioneering *Jugaad Innovation* by Navi Radjou, Jaideep Prabhu and Simone Ahuja. The many others whose work I have learned from are noted in the bibliography and references.

Much of the research for the book came through research projects supported by Michael Stevenson when he was running Cisco's education business. Other ideas and cases were drawn from research on innovation in education funded by Qatar Foundation.

Many people helped me research case studies in all parts of the world, from Africa and India to Brazil and Mexico: to them, thank you very much indeed. I am especially grateful to the many frugal innovators who spared their time and thoughts to help me, among them Mitch Besser, Madhav Chavan, Pedro Yirogen, Shannon May and Suresh Kumar, and Ayla Goksel, as well as other commentators in this field, such as Olivier Kayser at Hystra. My researchers on those projects – Annika Wong and Kate Stokes – were incredibly diligent and committed.

Eleanor Davey-Corrigan was vital to Palgrave Macmillan picking up the idea in the first place, while Tamsine O'Riordan and Josephine Taylor showed amazing patience and professionalism in seeing it through to its conclusion. Elizabeth Stone edited the manuscript with exemplary professionalism.

As ever, I could not have completed this book without the patience and understanding of my family and especially the constant support of my wife, Geraldine.

Preface: The Surfer and the Wave

Ideas that change the way we live and work are like waves. They start somewhere far off, out of view, and grow into a swell, taking in contributions from many different sources. As a wave builds up its momentum, it becomes more clearly part of a pattern of waves crashing onto the shore, with a rhythm, one feeding the other. Taking sole credit for any idea that really changes the world is like surfers claiming to have made the waves they ride. Surfers excel in reading the sea and spotting where the next big wave is coming from, knowing when to bide their time, when to shift position and when to make their move. The wave is more powerful than the surfer; yet the surfer shows what can be made of it.

This book is about a new wave of innovation that is spreading around the world. Frugal innovation is designed for and a response to its times: to make the most of the limited resources we have in order to create better, more successful and sustainable ways to live. Frugal innovation thrives on constraints, turning them to its advantage. Frugal innovation follows from something like a new economic equation:

Providing better solutions for more people by using fewer resources by doing things completely differently.

We need frugal innovation in many different industries and walks of life to allow us to face the immense, combined challenges of the next few decades: meeting the explosion of demand from billions of aspirational new consumers in the developing world; working within tight resource constraints on water, energy and carbon, imposed by climate change, scarcity and rising costs; providing a new model of growth for the majority of low- and middle-income families in the developed world who have seen their living standards stagnate. Meeting these challenges simultaneously will be possible only with a new model of innovation, one which creates better products, services and ways to live while using fewer resources.

The frugal innovators profiled in this book are among the first surfers of this wave. They come from far and wide; they tend to be both cosmopolitan in their ideas and outlook and yet also deeply rooted; they are committed to solving real-world problems that matter to them, where they live and work.

Devi Shetty in Bangalore has created the world's leanest low-cost hospital that provides heart operations at a fraction of the price of those in the developed world. Madhav Chavan and his team based in Mumbai found a way to educate pre-school children for just $10 a year. Suresh Kumar in Kerala invented a system of healthcare that relies on thousands of volunteers working with a tiny team of specialist doctors. Mitch Besser in South Africa found a way for HIV-positive women to counsel and mentor one another to improve their chances of taking anti-retroviral drugs. Pedro Yirogen in Mexico City has developed a mobile phone-based primary healthcare system used by 5 million Mexicans and which costs them just $5 a month. In Kenya Shannon May is growing a network of hundreds of low-cost schools, charging parents only $4.50 a month for an education that delivers far better results than much more expensive schools. In Australia and the Middle East innovators inspired by the ideas of British inventor Charlie Paton are creating water out of thin air, almost by magic, through desalination systems that use solar power. A team of Canadian-Indians, financed in the UK, are making the world's lowest-cost tablet computer, which performs as well as an original iPad but costs less than £40.

Many frugal innovators create their own organisations to make their innovations. But others work at established companies such as Tata and Unilever, Procter and Gamble and General Electric, which are now producing a string of frugal innovations. The Indian conglomerate Tata has produced the low-cost Tata Ace van, the iconic Tata Nano car and the Tata Swach low-cost water unit. Next it will launch itself into low-cost, prefabricated self-build housing that can be put together almost as easily as Ikea furniture. All over the world, in labs and design studios, a new generation of social designers is trying to create low-cost products that meet the needs of cash-strapped consumers, especially in the developing world. Many of them are adapting the mobile phones and the networks they run on to become, for example, banking infrastructures in Kenya and Pakistan or a test for anaemia or HIV. Meanwhile, a resurgent do-it-together movement of makers, hobbyists and craft producers is emerging, powered by the spread of low-cost digital technologies such as the Arduino motherboard, the Raspberry Pi computer and 3D printers. Advocates of this movement argue that it presages a new industrial revolution based on sustainable, local production, using local, recyclable materials. Many of the most important frugal innovations will not be standalone products and services but entire new systems for health, education, transport, energy and water. These systemic innovations will emerge from frugal cities around the world, which are inventing new ways for their citizens to sustain themselves. Singapore has solved a water crisis that threatened its future by turning itself into a giant, distributed, urban reservoir, recycling as much water as possible and desalinating seawater. Havana has learned how to feed itself from small plots within the city. Curitiba in Brazil recycles far more waste than comparable cities in the developed world, in large part thanks to an army of micro-recycling entrepreneurs. Freiburg in Germany has created new low-cost and shared approaches to housing and energy which make it possible for families on modest incomes to live well. A new generation of civic innovators, bringing together public and private sectors to solve complex problems, will create the frugal systems of the future that our cities need.

Although they come from many different sources, these early surfers of the frugal wave share some common features.

They make constraints work for them, forcing them to turn conventional wisdom on its head.

They regard being marginal as an advantage. They make the most of marginal markets, overlooked by large companies and where resources are scarce, to rethink traditional, costly, top-heavy business models.

They are unafraid to ask for the seemingly impossible and in the process sounding naive or even stupid. Charlie Paton asked whether it would be possible to make water from thin air using nothing more than the power of the sun. Gynash Pandey asked why it would not be possible for the poorest people to get electricity from the rice husks they throw away everyday. They do not mind posing questions that make them sound slightly mad.

They eschew cutting-edge technology. Instead, they prefer to do radical things with proven, often quite old-fashioned technologies, which are known to work, familiar to consumers and easy to maintain.

They are humble and unassuming rather than attention-seeking and arrogant. They welcome borrowing an idea from someone else and putting it to new use. They often do not invent anything at all, other than a way to take a solution to scale.

They excel at innovation as a process of 're'-thinking rather than as pure invention: they recycle, reuse, repurpose, remediate. They like nothing better than finding a new use for discarded, overlooked or wasted resources.

They cannot abide waste in any form. That is why they are disciples of the lean thinking first developed by Toyota in the midst of the crippling crisis that gripped the company after the Second World War.

When there is waste they turn it into fuel for another process. Were frugal innovators to become a political movement, their motto would be: waste is fuel.

Wherever possible they prefer simple, shared, social solutions. Simple solutions because they are easier to use, make and maintain. Social solutions because when people share an expensive piece of kit it makes it more affordable. Shared solutions help people to learn from one another.

Frugal innovations have four main common features: they are lean, simple, social and clean. The frugal innovators profiled in this book have created solutions with these four features, often over many years of trial, error and experimentation. The challenge is whether or not these principles can now shape and guide the development of larger companies, markets and systems and the lives of the consumers who use them.

Frugal innovation – the provision of better solutions, for more people, using fewer resources, by doing things completely differently – will not be the only approach to innovation in the future. But it will be the most important because it offers a way to create a successful, inclusive and sustainable economy. Make no mistake: the frugal wave is coming. It's time to start learning how to surf it.

chapter 1

Ask for the Impossible

Hospitals in India are performing heart and eye operations for a fraction of the cost of their equivalents in the West, and at a higher standard. A network of schools in Kenya has devised a way for children to be taught for $4.50 a month, petty cash to the public system, but it gets better results. About 5 million Mexicans use a primary healthcare service that they access through their mobile phones by paying a subscription of $5 a month. Researchers in Australia have invented a treatment for the most common cause of death among women who have just given birth – a treatment that can be delivered at home, by the woman herself, using a simple oral spray that costs a fraction of the traditional treatment. A city in Asia has worked out a way to provide itself with water by building a system of reservoirs beneath it so no rainwater is wasted, while a city in Central America has developed a way to feed itself by growing food on vacant lots.

All these solutions have been devised by a new wave of frugal innovators who are rewiring our economic operating system. If they succeed, so will we, because we will live and work in an economy that is less destructive, unstable, predatory and unequal. If they fail, then our future will be clouded by mounting conflicts over unequal access to scarce resources, especially in huge cities teeming with hot, hungry and angry young people disappointed that the promise of a better future has been betrayed.

The frugal innovators who will provide the solutions to the immense challenges we face in the next few decades are not the usual suspects. They do not wear hoodies and hang out in dorms at Harvard. They will not be found in the cafés of Palo Alto or in the gleaming research centres of large multinational companies in California. They will prefer to adapt tried-and-tested technologies rather than explore the unproven, cutting edge. Revolutionaries start with few resources, in the margins, outside the mainstream of power. These innovators are no different. They will be found operating under the radar, often in extreme conditions, armed with sparse resources to meet pressing needs. Their trick is that they make these severe constraints work to their advantage. They manage to achieve more, *because* they have less; they make their weakness work in their favour. As they lack the resources to afford traditional solutions they have no option but to turn conventional wisdom on its head: it does not work for the people these innovators serve and in the places where their consumers live. They work in places where doing what seems mad in terms of conventional wisdom instead becomes obvious. This new wave of innovators is drawing in people and ideas from around the world to devise new ways to provide clean water and decent food; affordable healthcare and low-cost housing; renewable energy and quality education. Not for them innovation as the baroque proliferation of functions, features, looks and styles. Their innovations are designed to meet people's most basic needs in new and more effective ways, doing a better job by doing it completely differently. At the core of the solutions they are coming up with are a set of design principles for products and services that set the template for successful products and services in future: they are *lean* and so they minimise all forms of waste; they are *simple* to be cheap to buy, low cost, easy to use and maintain; they are *clean* and so wherever possible they recycle and repurpose energy, materials and ideas rather than creating solutions afresh or using new resources; they create shared, *social* solutions because these approaches are usually more affordable. Above all they are frugal innovators: they do more *because* they have less, and because they have less they have no option but to think completely differently.

We will need the solutions they are coming up with because we face interconnected challenges of unprecedented scale and complexity. Business as usual will merely exacerbate many of these challenges rather than resolve them.

The economic growth model of the developed world is exhausted. The surest sign of that exhaustion was not the recession that followed the financial crash of 2008–9 so much as the mushrooming debt and financial irresponsibility which led to it. In much of the developed world the promise of rising living standards was kept alive only through financial smoke and mirrors. For most people the economy had already failed to deliver on its promise of steadily rising living standards long before the recession. The long, slow recovery from the crash is not a recession so much as a profound dislocation and disruption of established economic models. The developed world economies are looking for new models to provide sustainable growth which benefits the majority of their populations. All these economies are learning to live well with less.

Meanwhile, in the developing world hundreds of millions of people want access to the lifestyles of those in the developed world. The legitimacy of governments throughout the developing world, of all political stripes, rests on accommodating them. Meeting this demand from billions of new consumers for new televisions, cars, fridges, microwaves, houses, air conditioning and phones will not be possible within current models of production, but will tip the environment decisively towards potentially catastrophic changes and seriously aggravate growing conflicts over basic resources. Even if we were able to meet the demand of the next 2 billion middle-class consumers, this would still leave many millions more lacking clean water, reliable electricity, access to education, affordable housing. Using current models, many millions would be left behind in abject conditions, under-served and under-represented. All these pressures and challenges will be felt most intensely in the large, fast-growing cities of the developing world. These cities are where the 21st century will be won and lost. Each year 70 million people migrate to cities looking for a better future, arriving in places with housing, infrastructures and services that are woefully inadequate. Yet still they come. These cities, places such as

São Paulo and Dhaka, Istanbul and Lagos, will be where the future will be made as ingenious and determined people respond to the enormous constraints they face in creating a better life. If life in these cities can be made to work for the mass of the citizens with only modest incomes, then our future might be liveable. If new solutions do not emerge from and for these cities, then we could be in deep trouble.

This book is about where answers to these challenges will come from, the people who will devise those solutions and the methods they will use. These frugal innovators are generating clean local energy using recycled waste; growing food in cities and using solar-powered watering systems to dramatically reduce the energy involved; catching, recycling and cleaning water at low cost; providing access to basic health for millions for the price of a phone call; creating banking systems without banks; delivering education without schools and teachers; helping people to cope with disease, without doctors and hospitals. They will be innovators, but often not as we traditionally think of them.

Frugal innovators eschew the unproven, cutting edge of technology in favour of readily available, already proven, simple-to-use technologies that are known to work and which can be easily adapted to new tasks. They prefer services that work on robust second-generation mobile networks rather than experimenting with third- and fourth-generation services. They are not interested in the leading-edge, early adopters but in the mass of consumers with access to basic, low-cost technologies that are easy to learn how to use, cheap to acquire and simple to maintain. They like technologies that are simple, familiar and adaptable. They prefer solutions that are old, unsexy but reliable. They are inveterate tinkerers, they love DIY (do-it-yourself). But they really excel at DIT (do-it-together). Their forte is not pure creativity but innovation as a process of 're': *recycle, repurpose, reuse, recuperate.* They are re-innovators.

Frugal innovators do not confine themselves to technologies, products and services. They innovate organisations and business models, to mobilise resources and ideas in new ways. They will favour solutions that work with and can be used by consumers, enlisting their help to devise solutions, rather than just delivering to and for them. They can only work with consumers by staying close to them, understanding their lives. Like a guerrilla army, they operate among the people. They build organisations that resemble movements, encouraging people to make their own contributions to the organisation's goals. As organisations they are lean, clean and social: they draw on only the resources they need locally; they recycle as much as possible, often piggybacking on existing infrastructures rather than building them from scratch; they create shared forms of ownership and usage, to drive down costs; they parcel their products up in novel ways that poorer consumers can afford. Often they are financial as well as product innovators: they invent new ways for people to save and pay for products, whether through mobile banking or microcredit.

These frugal innovators cannot afford to be proud, arrogant and isolated. They have to be humble to borrow and generous to create shared solutions. They cannot afford to work in special, contrived environments, shiny innovation zones, cut off from the world around them. They have to innovate in the real world, in real time, learning rapidly by testing barely viable products with real consumers. They make the most of their marginality. They are not encumbered by being rich, powerful and professionalised. They are driven to innovate because they have very limited resources to respond to high aspirations and growing need.

Frugal innovators are like living oxymorons: they will have to make possible the seemingly impossible by providing better solutions while using fewer resources; and include many more in capitalism's embrace and yet reduce energy usage and the carbon footprint. That means creating a capitalism that is more socially responsible to help address basic social needs – for health, education, care, food, energy – on a vast scale, while also being far less wasteful and more environmentally sustainable, by husbanding resources more skilfully and thoughtfully. All this will require fundamental changes to our economic operating system. This book is about who they are, where they come from, how they work, the solutions they are devising to make our futures liveable and what business can learn from them.

In the next thirty years we face stark choices. We will prosper only if we embark on innovation on an unprecedented scale. What now looks impossible must become daily reality. That means the coming decades should be one of the most exciting times to be alive because radical new innovations which empower millions of people to live better lives should be emerging from all over the world. If this does not happen, then it may become one of the worst times to be alive as the constraints we face, compounded by deep inequalities in access to basic resources, will fuel conflict in an increasingly interconnected and technologically complex society. The following three chapters look at the three big changes to the context for innovation: the explosion of demand from billions of newly minted urban consumers in the developing world; the growing failure of developed world economies to deliver rising living standards for the majority; tightening constraints on resources imposed in part by climate change. These three factors create a new context and mission for innovation: to provide better solutions to basic needs using fewer resources. Chapter 5 starts to explore what all that means for innovation: how business develops new products and services and who for. Innovation has become almost a religion, a form of faith in the future. Yet innovation has increasingly become a force of proliferation, adding ever more products and features to lives already crowded with material possession. Innovation needs to be guided by an ethic of frugality – making a lot from a little. Frugal innovation is emerging from many different sources – from India and China, Brazil and Kenya; from grass-roots innovators but also from university labs; from big companies and small.

The next four chapters set out the four main ingredients of the frugal innovation playbook, to create solutions which are lean, simple, clean and social. Chapter 6 traces the lineage of lean solutions back to Toyota reinventing car production in power war Japan ravaged by severe resource shortages, and shows how lean thinking is being applied by frugal innovators in fields from health to education and energy. Chapter 7 explores why frugal solutions need to be simple, to cut out extraneous features, minimise consumer learning to adapt new products and provide end-to-end solutions. Chapter 8 argues that lean, simple, low-cost solutions will not be enough to meet out needs unless they are also clean. Using fewer resources will favour solutions that recycle, reuse and repurpose resources. Chapter 9 shows that frugal solutions are generally social because shared, and cooperative solutions are often more economic and creative. Chapter 10 draws together the threads of this analysis to provide a concise guide to the core ingredients of frugal solutions and frugal systems.

The method of frugal innovation is set out in Chapter 11, which explores the people, places and processes of frugal innovation: who does it, where and how. Chapter 12 examines how the lessons of frugal innovation from the developing world can be brought back to the developed world through reverse innovation flows. A new dynamic of global innovation is taking shape in which the ideas and technologies will flow through cosmopolitan networks of people and institutions. These international networks will be the most important focal points for frugal innovation, carrying ideas and solutions back and forth. Chapter 13, the conclusions, sets out the fundamental principles of frugal innovation: why we need it and how to make it central to innovation in companies, cities and government.

The Rush

Aziz Sagir sits intent and alert on a simple sofa in her bare apartment, her small face tightly drawn by her headscarf. In the densely packed Istanbul suburb of Esenler Merkez, the streets are so narrow it seems almost possible to touch the apartment buildings opposite. Aziz puts a protective arm around her four-year-old son Samet to encourage him to complete the worksheet that sits in front of them on a low table. He concentrates hard, keen to impress his mother; she responds by gently praising his efforts. The worksheet comes from a programme Aziz has enrolled in with about 20 other young mothers from the area, to prepare their children to go to school.

Aziz is in no doubt about what is at stake. She grew up in a remote Anatolian village, one of five siblings, and left school at the age of 12 to work in a market garden. Her frustration has turned into an implacable determination that her own children will not suffer a similar fate, their own potential stunted.

That sense of ambition and defiance leads Aziz each week to the cramped, windowless back room of a local community centre, where, with a group of other mothers, over a period of about six months, she learns how to prepare Samet to hold a pencil, make his letters, count in tens. They talk about what it means to be a good parent and how to deal with their errant husbands. Not one mother in the room went to school beyond the age of 12. All are determined to give their own children a better chance in life. That is why they have come to Istanbul.

These women are part of a social revolution that is unfolding daily, in hundreds of millions of ways in places like Esenler Merkez in cities across the world as people recently arrived from the countryside enter a daily renegotiation of who they are and what they are entitled to. Cities like Istanbul, Delhi and São Paulo are thronging with young people full of ambition. These young people are the future of capitalism, as workers, consumers, entrepreneurs and citizens. The incomes they earn will determine what they can buy and so what can be sold. What they want will be increasingly what is designed and made. These fast-growing cities, and especially the places where these young people first arrive and gather themselves, are where the future will be made.

The New Middle Class

That is a big shift in the centre of gravity for our economy and so for business and innovation. From the late 19th century through to the late 1970s, the driving force of consumption and innovation was the emergence, growth and rising affluence of what started as the industrial working class and became the mass middle class of Europe and the US. Their jobs, lifestyles and homes drove the focal points for consumption and so for business innovation. The mass markets for mass consumer products – fridges and televisions, cars and stereos, holidays and entertainment – were created around the aspirations and incomes of the workers employed in the factories and offices of large organisations. Innovation, the development of new products and services, was aimed at these consumers and the markets their demand created.

In the next few decades however, as the developed world economy seeks to shake off the persistent after-effects of deep recession, growth will increasingly come from new consumers, fresh to the market, in the developing world. Innovation will

Growth will increasingly come from new consumers in the developing world

increasingly have to focus on their needs, values and budgets. Underlying these shifts in consumer behaviour is a deeper, persistent social change.

In the past, for women like Aziz life was a condition they were born into, a fait accompli to be complied with. Their best option was to align themselves to what was possible within the narrow social confines of their lives, to move with the ebb and flow, but not to attempt to change course. Continuity and compliance were the keys to survival, not personal goals and achievements. Nowadays, gradually, people like Aziz are becoming able to step back from their own lives, to see them in a wider perspective, to compare themselves not just to their sisters and neighbours, but to people they see on television and through social media. They can see that their lives can be remade, albeit judiciously, and invested with their own meaning and purpose.

Each day across the developing world people in their millions, earning very modest incomes – of about $5,000 a year – wake up ready and excited for life to bring something new and different. Each day they loosen another notch in the ties that bind them to where they were born and instead seek to define who they are through what they do and what they own.

This social revolution is part of a shift from the older developed economies to the growth markets of Brazil and Russia, India and China, the BRICs, made famous by the Mancunian chief economist of Goldman Sachs, Jim O'Neill.[1] Like most big ideas that acquire a large following, O'Neill's is disarmingly simple: countries with large, young populations, eager to learn and work, freed from policy regimes and cultures that once held them back, will enjoy rising productivity and become major sources of economic growth. India has a young population of over 1 billion; China an older population of 1.5 billion; Brazil's population is 180 million and Russia's 140 million. The world economy has doubled in size since 2001 and a third of that has come from the BRIC economies, which have enjoyed a fourfold increase in aggregate GDP to $12 trillion. Some of that growth came as a by-product of serving the debt-fuelled boom in the US and elsewhere that pulled in exports. Yet in India most of this growth was domestically generated, and even in China domestic spending increased by close to $1.5 trillion in the past decade, roughly speaking the size of the entire UK economy.

Of course there are legitimate doubts as to whether this extraordinary growth story can continue. In 2013 some of these same wonder economies became known as the Fragile Five due to their vulnerability to shifts in US economic policy and exchange rates. Each of these economies faces huge challenges. In China the social and economic pressures of an ageing population, combined with the distorting effects of the one child policy, extremes of inequality and widespread corruption, feed political unrest. The past two decades of rapid growth in cities will bring in their wake a wide range of social dysfunctions and environmental problems in the next two decades. The very success of these economies is putting a brake on their growth, with rising wages eating into their competitiveness. They have not been able to escape entirely the impact of the recession in the developed world. Maintaining the extraordinary growth rates that many have come to see as normal may require policy-makers to take risks with inflation and debt.

Yet despite these evident risks, the big story is the sheer weight of numbers and momentum that will drive these emerging economies forward. By 2050 India could have a working population the same size as the entire population of the US. In China hundreds of millions of former peasants who have recently become city residents have only just begun to taste the fruits of urban life. Behind the BRICs stand other countries where governing elites realise their legitimacy will depend on delivering sustained improvements in living standards: Indonesia, Mexico, Turkey, Nigeria, Myanmar, Vietnam, the Philippines. O'Neill forecasts that 2 billion people will be brought into the global middle class between now and 2030, with incomes above $5,000 a year. By 2020 consumer spending in the BRIC economies may well outstrip that of the US.

These new consumers will throng into air-conditioned malls to seek the kinds of goods that are associated with affluence in the West. Audi is selling 2,000 cars a day mainly thanks to booming demand in India and China. In the cities of the developed world the first signs of this change are Brazilians buying apartments in South Beach, Miami, and timeshares in Vale; Chinese shoppers laden with bags in London's Bond Street and Tokyo's Omote Sando. Even in Hong Kong, the locals increasingly complain that upmarket stores are geared to Mandarin-speaking, cash-rich tourists from mainland China. Growth in the BRIC economies has come with extreme inequality: these economies have more billionaires than Europe despite having a much lower GDP, which means vastly more wealth is flowing into a much smaller number of hands. These shifts are a boon for US and European luxury goods makers like Chanel and Bentley. O'Neill's conclusion seems to be that new consumers of the developing world will make the same choices as those in the developed world. They will want the same things. But it is unlikely to be that simple.

Most of these new consumers will not make it to Western malls. They will have very modest incomes and some will have strong memories of living in villages; they will have been used to hoarding and reusing whatever they can; they will live in small dwellings, often with unreliable supplies of electricity and water. They will be both aspirant and resource-constrained. As a result they will drive a hard bargain. O'Neill and his colleagues at Goldman Sachs grow giddy at the thought of 500 million new consumers of luxury goods in the next 15 years, but far more significant might be the 1.2 billion who will have moved out of subsistence poverty by 2020. According to the World Economic Forum about 3.7 billion people are excluded from formal markets because their incomes are too low and fluctuating. They earn between $1 and $8 a day. Among this very large group about 1.1 billion, mainly in China and India, earn $2–$8 a day, and have just enough discretionary income to start buying more than essentials. Another 1.6 billion have incomes between $1 and $2 a day. These people on very low incomes are the next wave of mass-market aspirational consumers.

The affluent industrial working class, its cultures, habits and spending patterns made post-war capitalism in Europe and the US. This new wave, variously known as the Bottom of the Pyramid and the Next Billion consumers, is the wave to come. They are not, however, unthinking apprentices, eager to adopt, wholesale, a way of life that US and European consumers have already created. They often live in quite cramped conditions, so space is at a premium. Their incomes are not just low, but often fluctuate, and so saving, repaying debts and financial planning are big issues, especially when contemplating big-ticket items like household durables and home improvements. Their access to formal credit, from banks, may be limited. They are just as likely to use informal borrowing and savings schemes. As a result they may prefer to buy just as much as they need of an item rather than a large quantity. They may even prefer to share ownership with neighbours and family members to reduce costs. Reaching these consumers, often in slums and *favelas*, townships and shanties, crowded public housing or private rented blocks, is not always easy: they may not shop at superstores being fed by trucks despatched by sophisticated supply chains. People like Aziz do not generally travel very far: they tend to buy what they need from local suppliers they trust. They like products that are robust, reliable and often portable. They often lack the complementary infrastructures to make products work that Western consumers take for granted, such as clean water and reliable electricity. The iconic products for the mass consumers in the US and Europe of the 20th century sat squat like monuments in the corner of the room: the fridge, the washing machine and the television. For this generation of emerging consumers, in the developing world, the iconic product is simple and robust: a scooter or a mobile phone.

Paisa Vasool

On a hot and dusty road, with traffic locked and horns honking, on the edge of an Indian city that has stretched well beyond the bounds of its nominal infrastructure, a scrawny young kid draws up alongside a shiny Mercedes trapped in the traffic. 'Where do they all come from?' the plutocratic Merc driver mutters as he winds up his window in disdain. With a sneering glance at the guttersnipe prying eagerly into his car, he self-consciously readjusts his silk tie and fiddles with the Montblanc pen (standard issue for the Indian elite) sticking out from his top pocket. The boy on the bike, in a flash of defiance, whips a stick-on tie out of his satchel, smooths his ragged shirt and with a final flourish retrieves a biro from his bag and sticks it in his top pocket. Proudly he tells the Merc driver: 'It's just a matter of two more wheels; I'll get them.' Welcome to the world of New Rin, which in 2012 became India's fastest-growing washing powder by capturing the sense of boundless ambition and possibility among the newly emerging, motorbike-riding, biro-wielding consuming classes who excel at making a little go a long way.[2]

In India the drive to extract every last drop of value from a purchase is known as *paisa vasool*.[3] In most Indian households the housewife has to be a meticulous financial planner, saving everything possible to afford any large purchase. They are also ferocious bargainers. *Paisa vasool*, however, is not just about paying a low price for an item. It's also about making sure it is used to the full. That entails constant reinvention: shoes are resoled, shirts recollared, trousers passed from son to son. Nothing is thrown away in case it comes in handy. Old saris are reincarnated as quilts; ice cream pots grow plants, beds hide collections of plastic bags. For people brought up in conditions of scarcity, in the village and then the slum, running a tight ship and making the most of everything is absolutely vital. Indulgences have to be planned for. Even now, personal ownership is not a hard and fast idea in an Indian society where people can rarely command their own personal space and where people are used to living and sleeping in shared rooms with siblings. If one family gets an impressive piece of kit – a television – they quickly become a magnet for all and sundry, crowding round. Children get used to using computers together. The kinds of products that work in these conditions are robust, simple, portable and flexible. The scooter is a prime example: simple, modest, unflashy, imperfect but if necessary able to carry an entire family of five, everyone clinging to one another. The Indian auto-rickshaw travels at just the right speed for India's crowded roads. Like a shanty on wheels it is just adequate. These imperfect, just-good-enough solutions, that just about work, still abound in India. They are expressions of the practical, down-to-earth ethic of frugal design.

All of that might be swept away by the crisp, fresh and modern India that is being made in the burgeoning satellite cities of Gurgaon and Noida, in the new settlements with names like Rockwood and Belvedere, where non-resident Indians are lured to villas and mansions with manicured lawns and swimming pools. The rich of the new India are leaving behind all this 'make do and mend', bred by an economy throttled by bureaucracy and incompetence. In its place boundless consumerism is almost a symbol of national pride and achievement. Yet beneath the surface of the bright and shiny new consumerism, most of the emerging Indian middle class will have memories and habits of this shared, frugal, improvised approach, to wring every last drop of value out of what they buy.

Living on the Edge

The consumers who make up the next wave of capitalism will not all be found in gleaming shopping malls seeking out how to become just like people in the US and Europe. The conditions that many of these new consumers face remain very tough, by any standards. Take Pakistan, a country touted as a potential member of the next wave of growth markets, chiefly due to its proximity to India and its young population of 180 million, which is rising by 4 million a year. By 2025 there will be 60 million more Pakistanis. On paper Pakistan looks as if it could be another rising star and some parts of the country, in the Punjab, Lahore and Karachi, are thriving. Yet the supply of drinking water is a third per capita of that of India. The average Pakistani eats less than the average African. Electricity supplies are unreliable and depend on heavy government subsidy. Pakistan has enjoyed little of the boom in software and service jobs that has lifted incomes in parts of India: annual per capita income is $2400, putting Pakistan 179th in the world. The education system is failing to meet basic needs: Pakistan is one of the few countries in the world in which illiteracy is rising. To cap it all, Pakistan is highly vulnerable to climate change, from vicious floods pouring down from the mountains to rising sea levels in low-lying coastal areas. Many of the new consumers at the bottom of the pyramid find themselves in fragile states like Pakistan. The Organisation for Economic Co-operation and Development (OECD) estimates that about 1.5 billion people live in states that suffer recurring, often violent crises. These states are home to perhaps a third of the world's poorest people and attract more than 30 per cent of development assistance.

The most powerful driving forces of economic growth in the next half-century will be the turbulent and chaotic cities of the developing world.

The poorest and most disconnected parts of these cities – slums, informal settlements, low-income housing, ghettoes – will grow fastest. Urbanisation, the chief demographic force of the 20th century, will be even more powerful in the 21st century. In 1950 there were 86 cities in the world with more than 1 million inhabitants. By 2015 there will be at least 550. At least two-thirds of population growth since 1950 has been in cities. The majority of the world's population now lives in cities for the first time. In 1900 it was 10 per cent. By 2050 about three-quarters of a much larger world population will live in cities. Current trends imply the world's urban population will grow by 33 cities of 2 million inhabitants each year for the next 30 years, or 6 new megacities of 12 million people per year.

At least two-thirds of population growth since 1950 has been in cities

Developing world cities will grow fastest. Between 1990 and 2000 the urban population of the developing world rose by half a billion people to 1.9 billion. The combined urban population of China, India and Brazil is greater than the total population of Europe and the US. China has 97 city regions with a million-plus inhabitants and India 40. The US has 39. There are more million-plus city regions in Latin America (57) and Africa (41) than in Western Europe (40), the home of the civic city. Of the ten largest cities in the world eight are in the developing world – Mexico, Mumbai, São Paulo, Delhi, Kolkata, Buenos Aires, Jakarta and Shanghai. In 1950 developing countries accounted for 40 per cent of the world's urban population. By 2005 seven out of ten city dwellers were in the developing world. By 2030 it will be eight out of ten. Most of the new arrivals to these cities will live in informal settlements bereft of public services, far from work. Some slums count as megacities in their own right: Mumbai has 10–12 million slum dwellers, Mexico City and Dhaka 9–10 million, Lagos, Cairo, Karachi, Kinshasa, São Paulo, Shanghai and Delhi each have 6–8 million. Between them Karachi, Mumbai, Kolkata, Dhaka and Delhi have more than 15,000 registered slums with a combined population of almost 40 million.

Standing in the evening sun, as people pour back from Nairobi into the Kibera slum along the railway line built by the British, the atmosphere is almost carnivalesque. People shout and banter. Boys chase one another home from school, their satchels swinging. Fathers return from work carrying food for the family. People wearing the football shirts of teams from Britain and Italy abound. Surveying this scene, the daily migration of people from Kibera into Nairobi, two young women, Azra and Maureen, talk about their dreams. Azra wants to be a journalist; Maureen a civil rights lawyer. Both are hoping to go to college having finished their Kenyan Certificate of Secondary Education. Everything is stacked against them. Eleven families live in Maureen's small compound, sharing two-room homes, and a narrow courtyard where they cook on charcoal stoves and wash above a shared drain. Maureen shares her windowless home with her mother, father and four brothers. Her parents sleep on a mattress in the kitchen; the children sleep all together in the living room. There is no running water, nor sewerage. Electricity is available from illegal resellers. Clean water has to be bought. Maureen's mother works at a nearby hair salon, which, like most shops in Kibera, is little more than a shack. Her father tramps into Nairobi each day, along with thousands of others, looking for casual work. There is little prospect that they can afford the $1,000 a year Maureen needs to go to college. Families like Maureen's do not need Audi cars and Montblanc pens. They need basic services and reliable products that they can afford. The Kibera slum is a poor and often violent place but it can also be civic and social, almost like a village. Mobile phones and churches are plentiful. Industrial era infrastructures – pipes for water, cables for electricity, roads for cars – make little impression. Many of the new consumers the world over live in places like this, and if they do not, they have just escaped from them.

Yet despite the poverty, places such as this are incubators of a miraculous economic and social mutation as people newly arrived from the countryside become city dwellers. These places, which the Canadian journalist Doug Saunders calls 'arrival cities', are among the most overlooked and important places on earth: the places where people are absorbed through a porous membrane into the life of the city and so into modern jobs and markets.[4] This is where people get their foot on the first rung on the property ladder; where the first consumer durables are bought, often second-hand. Between 2007 and 2050 the world's cities will absorb an additional 3.1 billion people. To do so will require a wide array of innovations in several areas: housing, so people can build and own where they live; savings, so people can put aside a small part of what they earn to invest in the future; communications, so people can connect to the economic opportunities of the city (through mobile phones); education, so children can learn while parents work; shared transport to take people into the city in the form of shared taxi (such as the Turkish dolmus and the African mutatu); water systems to provide affordable, clean water, and energy systems that do not create clouds of pollution.

Jim O'Neill's account of the rise of the BRICs invites us to imagine millions of newly minted consumers pouring through malls with marble floors and sweeping up the cosmetics from the duty-free shop at Narita airport. Yet that will be true for just a richer minority. The overwhelming mass of new consumers will be relatively poor, with low and fluctuating incomes, and will live in informal settlements. Meeting the needs of these consumers will require products, services, distribution channels and business models designed to fit into their complicated and cramped lives. The kinds of businesses that succeed in these circumstances will require a new approach to creating products, one which has a sense of frugality – making a little go a long way – at its heart.

This shift represents both an immense challenge for established, mainly Western companies and a huge opportunity for those who can seize it. Doing so, however, will start with learning more about these new consumers, how they live and what they want. That will mean getting close to them and understanding their lives, values and aspirations. Many will want Western, branded products as symbols of their success. But that may only apply to products that are used to confer social status. These people are not slightly poorer versions of Western consumers who will be willing to buy slimmed-down versions of Western products. They want products that are well designed, and made with them in mind. That will often mean products that are robust, portable, effective and simple to use. These consumers are ferocious and ingenious in getting the maximum value from their modest incomes. They do not want second best or hand-me-downs. They want good products, designed for them, for homes that are small but horizons that seem endlessly to expand.

3

The Squeeze

The atmosphere on a crowded Virgin Pendolino train about to leave London's Euston station for the north-west of England is unmistakably tense. There is not enough space for all the people and the bags. Some people are already preparing to sit on the suitcases at the end of the carriage. Even those with seats feel squashed together. People without reservations are nervously occupying seats in the hope that their intended occupants will not arrive. The train may look sleek and aerodynamic but inside it seems to press in on the passengers; the walls seem too close, the ceiling too low, the aisle too narrow. As the train leaves London strange odours are already starting to waft from the toilets as people eye one another uneasily wondering what kind of travelling companions they will make squeezed together for the next few hours. The catering trolley, with its selection of over-priced pre-packaged food sold by a hard-pressed attendant, is yet to make an appearance.

This is what it will be like to live in Britain, and much of the developed world, for those on modest incomes for the foreseeable future: cramped, stuck, with little room for manoeuvre. People on middle incomes in the developing world may have recovered somewhat from the shock of the financial crash of 2008. They may no longer be scared. But nor are they especially hopeful and optimistic about their future. They will need to make sure their limited discretionary incomes go as far as possible. This is the second shift in the context for innovation: the sustained squeeze on the developed world's middle class.

From Need to Want

The economic history of the developed world since the Second World War can be divided into three main phases. The first phase, in the immediate aftermath of the war, was the era of need. People were focused on getting the basics, many of which were rationed, as they recovered from the disruptions and deprivations of wartime. The emphasis was on creating an infrastructure of basic, public goods: education and health, welfare and pensions, roads and homes. The collective institutions and state planning created in response to the depression, and which got the UK and the US through the war, still held sway. Taxes remained high; the public sector was large. Innovation came in the form of social and public mobilisation, to build homes for heroes and schools for their children. The war effort had underlined the role of science and organisation, scale and investment, to develop new technologies for jets and radar.

People did not see themselves as consumers, actively choosing between an array of options. They got by and made the most of what little they had. They consumed with restraint; there was little scope for conspicuous consumption. Those who did so were considered 'flash'.

By the early 1960s the second phase was gathering momentum. This was the era of want, when people started to see themselves not just as workers, citizens, professionals, mothers and husbands, but as consumers. In Shrewsbury, where I grew up, the arrival of this era was marked by the near-simultaneous arrival of a television, which brought us the first episode of *Dr Who*, a record player on which I listened to the Beatles sing in celebration of love and most tellingly a Safeway supermarket, all the way from the US, which announced itself with flamboyant red lettering. My mother took me for a visit to look in wonder at the aisles stacked high with a cornucopia of products we did not need and could not afford.

In those days, modernity arrived in leaps and bounds, with new products arriving fresh from modern production lines: a car and a fridge quickly followed the television and record player. The coal fires were replaced by gas and then the fires went altogether, to be replaced by central heating. Black and white gave way to colour as valves replaced transistors. It is not just the rosy glow of nostalgia which leaves the impression that these might have been the best of times for the majority of people on moderate incomes: the world was opening up to them, as their sons and daughters reaped the rewards of mass education by making their way to university and into better jobs. Orderly progress was evident everywhere in an economy supported and regulated by a state that seemed benign and intelligent, with business and unions incorporated into decision making. There was work for all; better food; larger, warmer houses; entertainments to lift our spirits and hospitals to mend our ills; greater social and geographic mobility, more choice and freedom of expression. But the frugal habits of making do had not disappeared entirely. Banks still controlled credit. Excessive spending was frowned upon. Yet everyone became more relaxed. All this was fed by a steady flow of new products, many of them from large US consumer goods companies: it was a time of Ford and Coke, Hollywood and Hoover. In 1955 just 18 per cent of UK households owned a washing machine; by 1975, it was 70 per cent. Television ownership over the same period rose from 19 to 96 per cent, while central heating spread from just 5 per cent of households to 47 per cent.[5]

From Desire to Frenzy

That golden era lasted little more than a decade before faltering in the 1970s as stagflation took hold. In the 1980s in the Anglo-Saxon world a critique of the golden era of ordered, fully employed economy emerged: the state was too big; taxes too high; trade unions too powerful; business too complacent; the consumer too constrained. In the US and the UK, this was the time of Margaret Thatcher and Ronald Reagan, of rising faith in privatisation, markets and individualism. The large US companies that had prospered in the 1960s found themselves under attack from upstart Japanese producers who were able to manufacture cars and electronic goods of higher quality and in more variety at lower costs. New retailers – Next and Benetton – started to remake a British high street long overseen by the paternalistic Marks & Spencer. Brands, styling, fashion and design started to make a larger impact. Liberal market reforms, in the US and the UK, boosted incomes and jobs, as the staid European economies seemed to languish. The UK economy appeared to regain its momentum and self-belief, as the consumer, homeowner and investor took the leading role. By the mid-1980s, those in work seemed to have loads of money and they knew how to spend it. Capitalism became more disorderly and impatient, as we became more visceral, hungry for a better deal, more choice, higher returns. Where once people might have saved a windfall for a rainy day, now they would spend it on a holiday.

The number of products available from increasingly flexible systems of manufacture and delivery multiplied enormously. The result was an extraordinary explosion in the number of products we could choose from.[6] The UK food industry introduced 1,030 new products in 1970; this nearly doubled to 2,016 in 1980 and reached 9,192 in 1990. By this time 2,000 new beverages were introduced in a single year. In the early 1990s more than 20,000 new lines were being introduced into UK supermarkets each year. Brands that had once survived by making just a single product embraced this proliferation. By the early 1990s Crest and Colgate were producing no fewer than 35 different kinds of toothpaste. Milk that once came in pint bottles started to come as semi-skimmed, skimmed, lactose-free, soya and microbiotic, in a wide variety of sizes of containers. No one drinks milk anymore; they drink a kind of milk. The post-war ethos of collectivism, sacrifice, denial and conventionality, gave way to aspiration, desire and eventually the pursuit of individuality, self-expression and self-fulfilment through consumption. At the start of the 20th century the average family might expect to have very little done for it other than by local suppliers of services. By the end of the century the average family could expect, on tap, an array of goods and services delivered to its door to suit its every need. The heirs to the high street revolution started in the 1980s were Wal-Mart and Tesco, Zara and H & M.

Some time in the mid-1990s, this culture of want and desire tipped over into the third phase: a kind of frenzy. The explosion of choice delivered by increasingly sophisticated retailers and increasingly flexible production networks, combined with other factors to create this frenzy. The opening up of China as the world's factory created a seemingly bountiful source of ultra low-cost products: we could consume more, without risking higher inflation, because spare capacity on a vast scale was being brought into production in the Far East. That coincided with a surge of innovation and creativity from the cosmopolitan entrepreneurial networks of high-tech clusters such as Silicon Valley. Despite the ups and downs, the bubbles and the bursts, these tech-entrepreneurs and their venture capitalists brought to us another seeming miracle: digital products that shrunk every year and yet provided more power, at lower cost. Taken together this was an unprecedented double dose: consumers were able to get more for less, without even trying. The advent of Internet shopping and home delivery meant that just after the beginning of the 21st century a middle-class family could have virtually anything delivered to its door including the weekly groceries. The final actor, however, administered an overdose: the financialisation of the economies of the developed world.

As consumerism became increasingly hedonistic, so savings ratios fell and credit expanded, in a bewildering variety of forms, to give consumers the impression of more wealth and greater spending power. Advocates of financial innovation argued that as we became better at understanding and calculating risk, then the more markets would work with complete information and so the better they would allocate risk and raise productivity.

Financial Froth

Every aspect of the economy became overlaid with a complex financial superstructure that bore little relation to underlying economic activity. Interest rate derivative trading grew from next to nothing in 1980s to

$390 trillion in 2009. Oil futures trading increased from 20 per cent of global production and consumption in 1980 to ten times that in 2010. Foreign exchange trading rose from 11 times the value of global trade in 1980 to 73 times in 2009. Interest rate swaps only started in the 1980s and were worth about $385 trillion in 2008. Collateralised debt obligation (CDO), which allowed mortgages to be parcelled up into different levels of risk, became a way for originators of mortgages to pass on bad loans without taking responsibility for the consequences. About $5 billion CDOs were issued in 1996.

After the Second World War, in the era of need, patience and prudence had the upper hand. People were used to waiting for what they wanted. Mostly they bought what they needed to get by. Shopping yielded occasional, restrained pleasures but it was not a route to self-fulfilment. In the second period, the era of want ushered in American goods and styles (but made real by Japanese production systems), and the desire for better homes, kitchens, cars, holidays, clothes, food, became the driving force of the economy. People improved themselves through consumption. In the 1990s these appetites became more visceral as horizons shortened. Hedonistic pleasures were easy to identify, package and sell and so desire gradually gained the upper hand.[7] In the third period, this turned into a frenzy of innovation in products, technologies, brands, lifestyles and finance. Innovation brought a quickening flow of new and cheaper products and services, designed in California, made in China and financed by Wall Street. Not only did those opportunities for consumption arrive at a faster rate but the disciplines of self-control that were in place in the 1950s and 1960s were being dismantled by a finance sector intent on providing people with more credit, often on the basis of the rising value of their homes. The compelling products of innovation, beautifully styled and duly branded, made it harder to stick with what you had, especially when your friends and colleagues were busy disposing of older models and upgrading to new ones. Investments in patience, self-control and discipline are difficult and costly at the best of times, but at the height of the frenzy in the late 1990s and early 2000s, it seemed almost impossible to be happy with what you had. The speed at which we could please ourselves far outpaced our ability to exercise self-control, to defer gratification until we were sure we could afford it.

This era of frenzy was fed by a kind of orgy of innovation. It came to a shuddering halt in 2008, with the financial crash.

The next phase of capitalism in the rich world is still taking shape as the developed economies and the majority of their middle-class consumers struggle to emerge from the dark tunnel of the Great Recession. A different consumer culture is taking shape. This culture is what will drive innovation in future.

Squeezed, Cramped and Uncomfortable

It is not just that consumers are spending less, saving more and relying less on credit. The recession has compounded an even more fundamental, long-run development: for the majority of middle-class consumers the link between the growth of the economy and the growth of their income and wealth has broken down. The era of mass aspirational affluence, which drove capitalism in the second half of the 20th century, is over. A different kind of consumer satisfaction will emerge in the years to come, one more suited to the straitened circumstances people find themselves in. If innovation becomes narrowly focused on the elite of rich consumers who can afford to buy the latest gadgets, made by the top brands, then it will bypass the majority. That would mean that innovation, the main engine of capitalism and growth, would not be serving the needs of the majority but catering for a rich minority. That is a recipe for capitalism gradually losing its chief source of legitimacy: its ability to deliver improving living standards for most people.

The Great Recession is responsible only for a part of this shift in consumer culture: unemployment has risen almost everywhere and employment fell for a long period. Across much of the developed world overinflated house prices have been flat or falling and public spending has been cut back to reduce deficits. The trauma of the Great Recession and its aftermath, however, is just the presenting symptom of a deeper chronic condition: the stagnation of incomes for the majority of people in many developed economies. It is this stagnation and its implications that business needs to understand.

From Frenzy to Stagnation

This stagnation has been most prolonged and pronounced in the US where incomes for many male unskilled workers have barely risen in the past three decades, despite periods of strong economic growth. Household incomes have increased, despite male wages flatlining, in large part due to rising women's employment. Now that surge is running out of steam and many households find they can only just make ends meet with both parents working. That in turn means families are dependent on often expensive childcare arrangements which put parents and grandparents under huge strain. Faith in the American Dream is starting to ebb as middle-class Americans get bogged down. Compared with their parents' generation they still feel rich. Compared with how they were doing two decades ago they feel they have made little progress. Their optimism for their children's generation is muted.[8]

A 2012 study by Pew Research found that 85 per cent of people who self-identified as middle class said they were finding it much more difficult to maintain their standard of living. As Pew concluded: 'Since 2000 the middle class has shrunk in size, lost out in income and wealth and shed some – but by no means all – of its characteristic faith in the future.' Four in ten households said their finances were in worse shape than they had been a year earlier and half of those estimated it would take at least five years to get back on an even keel. That came after a decade in which mean family income fell, especially for the middle class. While people on higher incomes – more than twice the median – enjoyed rising wealth, despite the crash, the middle classes became markedly poorer. By 2010 the net worth of the average middle-class American household was back where it was in 1983: about $93,000. The five years from 2007 wiped out all the gains in wealth the middle classes had made over the previous 15 years.

The US is not alone. In the UK median incomes have been faltering since the late 1990s. In the five years before the Great Recession, when GDP expanded 11 per cent, median male earnings fell. A forklift truck driver in the UK, working in a highly automated warehouse, was paid £19,068 in 2010, about 5 per cent less than his equivalent in 1978.[9] The Office of Budget Responsibility estimates that wages could be lower in 2015 than they were in 2001. The Resolution Foundation, a think-tank specialising in researching the incomes of the middle class, forecasts that a male full-time worker on low to middle income will earn less in 2020 than in 2003. Similar trends are at work, perhaps less viciously, in other countries. In Canada median male incomes have barely risen for 20 years and in Germany for 10 years.

The reasons for this stagnation are deep-rooted. Wages have been under pressure from global competition. New technologies have rewarded higher-skilled workers and displaced many more routine, manual jobs. In some places a low-productivity, low-wage retail and service economy has emerged, where the so-called 'precratariat' are employed on part-time and flexible contracts. The share of economic growth that goes to workers and wages rather than investors and capital has fallen. The richest people have made the greatest gains from this shift, especially in the US and the UK: the richest 1 per cent of Americans earned 34 per cent of all income from investments in 1980 but 65 per cent in 2005. Growth alone is not a solution to the crisis of the middle class. Even if economic growth were to return to pre-recession levels, it would not materially benefit those on median incomes.

Growth alone is not a solution to the crisis of the middle class

The middle class is being further squeezed because it has to pay for more out of those limited incomes. Inflation is higher for those on median incomes because more of their incomes go on basic goods – energy, transport and food – for which there are few substitutes. In the UK childcare costs are often crippling for families, so that even households with both parents working find it hard to make ends meet. People preparing for a longer old age find employers' contributions to pensions are being cut and their own savings will have to rise to compensate. Meanwhile cuts to public services will particularly hurt those on modest incomes, who are not poor enough to qualify for state support and not rich enough to be able to afford private provision. All of this will further constrain the already limited discretionary income of the middle classes.

Many families managed to avoid this economic reckoning only thanks to an apparently virtuous circle that linked borrowing, credit and rising house prices. In the UK, for example, the household debt to income ratio rose from 93 per cent in 1995 to 143 per cent in 2010. As house prices rose so people 'withdrew' equity to borrow more, from flexible, open and welcoming financial markets. That allowed people to increase their spending despite flat incomes. In 2008, about 8 per cent of the equity held in houses was 'withdrawn', the highest level since records began, to supplement stagnant incomes. In the US, middle-class debt rose faster than housing equity in the run-up to the crash.

That cycle has gone into reverse. In economies where there was a housing boom – the US, Ireland, Spain – house prices have fallen sharply, leaving many bankrupt, or at best with negative equity. In the US the net worth of middle-income families dropped 39 per cent in the later years of the decade as the housing market crash and Great Recession wiped out the previous advances. From 2007 to 2010 the middle classes tried to pay off their debts but found their houses losing value more rapidly: mean debt level for middle-income families fell 11 per cent, or $11,040, but the value of their assets fell even more, by 19 per cent, or $75,621.

The Zombie Economy

Where house prices have not fallen by so much, another problem has emerged: young people on modest incomes, in insecure jobs, now find it impossible to get on the housing ladder as it has become so much more difficult to get a mortgage. Housing, the traditional route to wealth for many middle-class families in the UK, is now not an option for many. Greater numbers of adult children are living with their parents and renting is becoming much more common. Meanwhile people on median incomes who do own homes find that even with low interest rates a very large share of their income is going on mortgage payments. Many are like economic zombies: just able to pay the interest on their debts but not in a position to pay off any of the capital. Many were only able to become homeowners thanks to 100 per cent mortgages. Should the economy pick up, and inflation and interest rates rise, then many households could find these repayments crippling. Even if these households have some nominal equity in the value of their homes, they will find it harder to borrow against that collateral.

In much of the rich world, this vicious cycle of incomes, living standards, housing and credit is complicated by another, even more fundamental factor: an ageing population. The fastest-growing age groups in many countries are those over the age of 65 and in particular over the age of 80. Families and governments will have to put more resources into pensions, health and social care. Younger taxpayers, with constrained incomes and in more insecure forms of employment, will find their taxes paying for the care of older people, some of whom will be sitting on very valuable properties but unable to do much with their wealth.

The Great Recession marks a turning point for societies in the developed world. It is not just that the recession has had a catastrophic impact on unemployment and incomes for those with low skills. The ill-judged and self-interested financial risk-taking that led to the crash fed debt to economies that would otherwise have felt stagnant. That sense of stagnation can no longer be disguised. For most of the second half of the 20th century, middle-class culture was aspirational and optimistic, looking forward to a procession of improvements: larger, more comfortable homes and cars; better educated children with more promising job prospects; long and comfortable retirements; holidays in places with reliable climates. For at least the next two decades the developed world's middle class, the engine of innovative consumption and lifestyles, will live subdued, slower, quieter lives. The era of the self-confident, affluent, middle-class consumer is coming to an end.

This more subdued and precarious middle class will have to save more to pay down debt and prepare for their old age. They will have less discretionary income and so they will search far more actively for good value. For many that will mean searching out low-cost products and solutions – low-cost airlines, own label detergents, discounted household basics. They may, however, be prepared to spend heavily on products that have a strong emotional appeal or which will last longer because they are well designed. The providers of these products will have to work harder than ever to establish the value they provide, especially as consumers increasingly use tools available through the mobile Internet to search and compare prices, performance and user ratings. The 'loads of money' conspicuous consumption of the 1980s and 1990s, dominated by fashionable brands, is giving way to a pride in being an inconspicuous, careful and clever consumer who makes the most of limited resources. Middle-class consumers will respond to stagnant incomes by becoming more resourceful: adopting their own version of *paisa vasool*.

Minimalism and Pay Day Loans

In some places this is leading to a reassessment of consumer culture itself. In the US a small but influential group of 'simplicity' bloggers are promoting a self-help movement of mindful, minimalist lifestyles, in which people learn to live well with less by foregoing high-pressured jobs and excessive consumption. Ryan Nicodemus and Joshua Field Millburn, the self-styled 'minimalists', urge people to create more and consume less; then learn to take pleasure in giving; to value relationships and to take the time to savour experiences.[10] Leo Babauta, the author of the bestseller *The Power of Less*, and Courtney Carver, in *Be More with Less*,[11] urge people to see that 'stuff is just stuff' rather than a source of fulfilment; to share ownership and learn to live with enough rather than in the land of plenty. All of them stress that the most valuable things in life – love, friendship, care, trust – are free and come from relationships, not things. The minimalists are in a minority but their calls for a slower, better, way of life echo those of the slow food and downshifting movements that started more than a decade ago. They touch a nerve.

Mindful minimalism, reinventing simple virtues of thrift and patience, is however just one expression of a new, constrained consumer culture.

Our high streets reveal another side of the story: the rise of pawnbrokers and pay day loans, pound stores and food banks. The most innovative financial services company in the UK to emerge from the recession is Wonga, a mobile phone-based pay day loan service. If a customer keeps a Wonga loan for six weeks they would be paying interest of 4,000 per cent. Most consumers are probably not becoming minimalists so much as better shoppers, through online shopping, the use of discount coupons and price comparison websites. The pressure from these has led to the closure of middle-ground high street retailers in the UK such as the music store HMV, the video chain Blockbuster and the camera shop Jessops. The companies that will grow in these conditions will deliver demonstrable value at reasonable prices, with high levels of quality, decent design and convenient service.

The majority of middle-class households in the post-war era felt buoyed-up by a rising tide of affluence. Now for many in the middle class it feels as if the tide is receding, leaving them marooned. The middle classes find themselves having to relearn the lost art of self-control, patience and prudence, in which consumption is planned and deferred until it is earned. They cannot afford to be impulsive and myopic. This is the new norm for middle-class consumers and they will be looking for products and services that help them make the most of their cramped conditions.

Innovation Out of the Squeeze

This shift in the nature of middle-class life represents a sea change in the conditions for innovation. The rich plutocrats, the top 5 per cent of wage earners, will still demand shiny, new, branded products, in the latest styles and with a rich array of features. However, most consumers will be looking for something different. They will want products and services that help them balance the demands of prudence and pleasure, to mix self-control and self-expression.

Economic growth in the developed world increasingly benefits the very rich while leaving everyone else pretty much at a standstill. The fundamental design flaw in contemporary capitalism is its failure to generate a collective sense of hope: the dimming of the American Dream of endless aspiration; the loss of faith in the European idyll of a more communitarian, cohesive social capitalism; Japan's lost decades of close-to-zero growth; the growing strains in the high tax welfare states of the Nordic countries. The heart of that design flaw is the growing disconnection between economic growth and the hopes of the majority of people. That disconnection will spread gloom and despondency, fear and anxiety, unless it can be reframed as an opportunity for innovation on a massive scale, from education and health, to social care and transport, to glasses and computers, to household appliances and cars, to help people to live more successful lives with fewer resources.

Innovation is at the heart of capitalism's adaptability. Yet innovation needs to be recast and rethought. That means not just new places and practices of innovation but also a new ethic, less about a proliferation of products and features, more about meeting basic needs well.

Scarborough, a seaside town in North Yorkshire in the UK, is an unlikely place to go looking for such an ethic. Scarborough was where my Great Auntie Mabel lived. When declining an extra helping of food she would say: 'No thank you. I have an ample sufficiency.'

The word ample has a pleasing ring to it, implying something that is filled out and well rounded. Yet ample would not do on its own. Auntie Mabel added the idea of sufficiency to show that what she considered ample was not just a question of how much food she wanted. It was a matter of how much she needed. What she had on her plate was ample because it was sufficient. Through this convoluted phrase my Great Auntie Mabel, one of a family of dissenting Methodists who came to pleasure uneasily, negotiated the relationship between what she wanted and what she needed. She was not enslaved to her appetites. She wanted to live well but within her means.

In many respects my Great Auntie Mabel's ethic for choosing how much food to have on her plate and how to live life well is one that might serve well as the ethic for our times: learning to enjoy an ample sufficiency;

learning to make the most of solutions that may not be the height of luxury but will be both good and enough. In the decades to come, we will need innovations that are well designed to be good because they are enough.

The lesson for business is that we are now in a very different phase. The squeeze on the cramped middle classes can no longer be relieved through financial engineering. To live well, middle-class consumers in the developed world will need well-designed products that help them make the most of their straitened circumstances.

chapter **4**

The Crunch

In the 20th century industrial capitalism pulled off an amazing trick. It used more resources than had ever been used in human history – coal, iron ore, oil, water – to create more products for more people and yet at the century's end prices of basic resources were 50 per cent lower than they had been in 1900.

In the present century we will have to pull off an even more staggering trick: to create goods and services for an even larger middle class – rising from perhaps 1 billion to more than 4 billion people – while attempting to limit a potentially catastrophic rise in global temperatures and using basic commodities that may well become more difficult and costly to acquire. The resource-intensive capitalism of the past century will lead us to disaster and conflict in the present century. Acquiring the minerals, commodities, land and water to meet this surge in demand will, on current trends, lead to further alarming environmental degradation and bring in its wake social turmoil, not least caused by rising and volatile prices for energy, food and water. Denying hundreds of millions of people lifestyles they aspire to will further entrench inequality and fuel social discontent. Yet meeting this demand using current technologies and production processes will edge us towards disaster. Reconciling these pressures will require a wave of sustained innovation and creativity on an unprecedented scale, in how we acquire and use resources to power our offices and factories, heat our homes, grow our food and move about. The next 30 years will have to be an era of unparalleled creativity to innovate new ultra resource-efficient ways to live and work. Without it we could be in deep trouble.

The prospect has excited those of deeply pessimistic outlooks, the most polemical of whom is Stephen Emmott, the computer scientist whose controversial book *10 Billion* predicted there was no hope of averting environmental and social disaster brought on by overpopulation.[12] There is no known means to feed 10 billion people at current rates of consumption and using current methods of production, Emmott argues, without causing environmental catastrophe. Attempts to meet rising demand for food using current technologies will just push us further and quicker into crisis: more land and water taken over for food production will only exacerbate climate change. Meeting rising demand for energy would, Emmott claims, require 18,000 more large dams, 23,000 more nuclear power stations and 36 billion solar panels, using current technologies. He entirely discounts the possibility of widespread behavioural change, as we adapt to different circumstances and innovation to provide more effective solutions. There is no sign, he argues, of any serious effort being made on either front: we are accelerating towards disaster. His book concludes with a gloomy prediction that the future will be a war of all against all as people compete violently to protect what little they have. Teach your children to use a gun, is the best advice he can offer. The best thing about Emmott's book is that it is very short. Critics complain it is strewn with errors, dependent on graphics lifted from the Internet which are misinterpreted, engages in careless exaggeration, ignores contrary evidence and neglects important innovations that provide solutions.

Yet in one respect Emmott is right. The biggest experiment in the world is not being conducted at CERN by scientists using the Large Hadron Collider; it is the experiment we are all engaged in daily to find out how to live together on a planet with 10 billion people. To find a solution we will need not just inventiveness, but to turn on their heads the conventional approaches that have got us this far. Not everyone who thinks we face a huge environmental challenge shares Emmott's pessimism. A more thoughtful view comes from Hans Rosling, the Swedish public health specialist, who argues that the absolute size of the world's population is less important than how we choose to live together. In a more equal world, in which resources were distributed more fairly, there might be more than enough to go around. There is still enough water in the world to meet all our needs – it's just in the wrong places – and consumers in the rich world take too much by spending too long in the shower and eating too much meat, the production of which requires large inputs of water. The kinds of innovations Rosling has in mind are frugal – lean, simple, clean and social. This is the environmental case for why we need such innovation.

Leaping Forward

In the 20th century we decisively broke our dependence on energy systems that were fed by the wind and sun and which we supplemented with human and animal muscle power. That leap was made possible by innovations that allowed us to extract, pump, use and transform raw materials, particularly to unlock energy stored in coal and oil, to make chemicals and plastics. That in turn allowed a massive expansion in population, lifespans and economic growth. The rise of industrial capitalism from 1851 to 1971 went hand in hand with a surge in population, mainly in cities, provided with better food and public health.[13]

One measure of the 20th century is the way humans started to use resources for their own good, to breed larger populations and live longer, richer lives. Take coal as an example. Annual global coal production was about 10 million tonnes in 1880, 762 million tonnes in 1900 and 5,000 million tonnes in 1990. Oil production was 20 million tonnes in 1900 and 3,000 million tonnes 90 years later. World energy use went from about 1,900 million tonnes of oil equivalent in 1900 to 30,000 million tonnes in 1990. We have deployed more energy since 1900 than in the rest of human history combined. In the 100 centuries between the dawn of agriculture and 1900, people used only two-thirds as much energy as they did in the 20th century.

Much the same extraordinary story can be told about our use of timber, minerals, fishstocks, soil and fresh water. In 1900 we drew down about 580 square kilometres of fresh water, much of it for agricultural irrigation; a century later it was 5,190 square kilometres, mainly to grow food for larger urban populations. In 1920 there were about 300,000 tractors in the world; by 1990 there were 26 million, tilling land more intensively to produce food for a population expanding at the rate of a city the size of New York every month. Producing food for this population on an industrial scale has led to extraordinary erosion of soils that took centuries to create: an area seven times as large as Texas is now irreversibly degraded by topsoil erosion. The US loses 1.7 billion tonnes of topsoil a year.

The environmental balance sheet of the last century reads like this: the population of humans and cattle rose fourfold; the pig population rose by a factor of nine, as did our water use; urban population expanded 13 times; the world economy grew 14 times larger and industrial production by a factor of 40; energy use rose 16 times; the fish catch rose 35 times; sulphur dioxide emissions went up 13 times and carbon dioxide 17 times. In 1900 we emitted 5,300 tonnes of copper and 47,000 tonnes of lead into the atmosphere; by 1990 those figures were 47,000 and 340,000 respectively. The US produces 12 billion tonnes of solid waste a year. New York alone produces 10,000 tonnes a day.

Remarkably, through this massive mobilisation of natural resources, prices for energy, food, water and steel fell. The more we used, the lower the prices went. Despite a fourfold increase in global population, a twenty fold increase in economic output and rises in demand for resources ranging from 600 per cent to 2,000 per cent, a basket of representative basic commodities cost 48 per cent less at the end of the century than at the start, according to an analysis by the McKinsey Global Institute.[14]

When this process got started nature may have seemed alien, untamed, vast and bountiful, full of virgin land and free materials. There was little reason to worry about the earth's capacity to first provide these resources and then to wash away and absorb the waste created in the process. No more. Many of the natural systems we depend upon are in a fragile and precarious state.

That means the productive systems of the *near* future will have
to be built on a respect for our interdependent relationship
with the natural world. The resource-intensive, profligate
economic model of the 20th century cannot be
sustained in the years ahead.

Many of the natural systems we depend upon are in a fragile and precarious state

Precarious Margins

The best known reasons for that are the already pressing demands of climate
change. Forecasts of likely global warming are clouded in controversy and
uncertainty; however, recent increases in greenhouse gas concentrations
have led scientists to predict that temperatures could increase by between
1.3 and 4.3 degrees centigrade above pre-industrial levels.[15] Warming on
this scale could lead to substantial and damaging changes in ecosystems
and weather patterns, including severe droughts, hurricanes and rising sea
levels. A 2013 survey of Arctic sea ice showed a record decline to just half
the level it was in 1979 when measurements began. Efforts to combat
climate change will focus on reduced consumption of resources, especially
energy and carbon. The Stern Review of climate change, commissioned by
the British government, predicted that adjusting to climate change would
cost the equivalent of 1 per cent of global GDP, which would cost each
person on the planet $104 a year.[16] If confined to consumers in the rich
world, the costs would be $667 per resident of the OECD – a reduction
in spending power in the US equivalent to a 10 per cent increase in the
inflation rates.

That task will be made all the more difficult as billions of people start
new lives as middle-class consumers, especially in China and India. China
will be about as rich per capita by 2040 as the US is now. If China then
matches US levels of car ownership there will be 1 billion more cars on
the road, almost doubling world car usage. If Chinese consumers eat meat,
milk and eggs in the same quantities as people in the US, according to
eco-statistician Lester Brown they will consume 1.352 million tonnes of
grain, or two-thirds of the world grain harvest in 2004.[17] They would use

99 million barrels of oil a day, 20 million more than we produce at the moment. If China's coal burning were to reach current US levels – nearly 2 tonnes per person – then the country would use 2.8 billion tonnes annually, more than the current world production of 2.5 billion. China already uses more steel than the US even though its urbanisation is far less advanced. A China modelled on US levels of consumption and production would require 303 million tonnes of paper a year, double current world production. If China consumed as much seafood per capita at Japan then it would require 100 million tonnes of fish a year, more than the world's entire current catch which has already brought many fisheries to the point of collapse. That is just China. With India and the rest of the developing world following rapidly in its wake, the growth in demand will put unsustainable pressure on our natural systems. The Global Footprint Network estimates that we are already consuming resources equivalent of 1.5 planets and we would be consuming the equivalent of 4.5 planets if everyone matched US patterns of consumption.[18] This is all despite the fact that perhaps 1.3 billion people lack access to reliable electricity and 884 million do not have safe drinking water. Even with billions lacking basic amenities, the rest of us are consuming too much for the earth's good.

The scale of our growing call on natural systems is pushing many to the point of no return. The UN Millennium Ecosystems Assessment, compiled by a panel of 1,300 scientists, found that 'human actions were depleting the earth's natural capital, putting such strain on the environment that the ability of the planet's ecosystems to sustain future generations can no longer be taken for granted'.[19] When natural systems are so fragile that they cannot reliably reproduce themselves, then quite small changes can tip them into a critical spiral of decline that becomes impossible to reverse. A small increase in fishing by historic standards can suddenly trigger a precipitous collapse in oceanic fisheries. Many of the ecological buffers we have relied on in the past – open land, unused water, unpolluted spaces, untapped stocks of resources – that helped societies weather difficult times, are going or gone. We are living on increasingly precarious margins. Like a team of climbers on a ledge roped together, every move counts. Apparently free and plentiful natural resources also provided social and economic buffers. As resources become more precious and we become more interdependent, so the likelihood of conflicts over scarce resources, especially water, will become more intense. Competition over resources, combined with displacement of population by floods and droughts, will put already fragile social systems under increased strain. The first signs of this are already evident not in the rich parts of the world but in the poorest. Take Uganda as an example. In 2006, after two years of drought, the water level of Lake Victoria dropped a metre. That meant less water was available to fuel the generation of electricity at the Owen Falls dam. This led to rationing of electricity and higher prices as the government turned to more expensive thermal sources. The consequence was that many households could not afford electricity for cooking and so increased their use of firewood, which in turn accelerated deforestation, which contributed to the degradation of land and soil, leading to lower food yields.

The Canary in the Mine

In an age of severe resource constraints the canary in the coal mine is Pakistan, where on any one day stories about rising food prices, electricity blackouts and water shortages jostle for attention with those about suicide bombings, corruption and political strife. The population of Pakistan will grow by 60 million by 2025, at which point the population will be growing at 4 million people a year. Pakistan has few natural resources and only 0.32 acres of arable land per capita. That will fall by a third unless new land is brought into production, itself a costly process. As a result Pakistan is likely to be a heavy food importer but lacks the natural resources, oil and gas, of its neighbours to afford the imports. Pakistanis already have only a third of the fresh water of India and eat no more than they did on average in the 1970s. Wood and other biomass still account for 46 per cent of energy use: it's a common sight in Islamabad on a Friday night to see men cycling home with huge bundles of foraged firewood on the handlebars of their bikes. Competition for water supplies will be as big a threat to the future of Pakistan as militant Islam. Pakistan, a nuclear power, could become a nightmare of political and environmental instability.

The consequence of these mounting pressures on resources will be rising and more volatile prices for commodities, which are increasingly interlinked. Food production relies not just on water but energy, for fertiliser, to pump water from deeper reservoirs and to transport food to markets. The first decade of the 21st century saw sustained and sharp rises in the prices of basic commodities: energy prices rose 190 per cent and food by 135 per cent. Of course commodity prices have peaked before, most recently after the oil shocks of the 1970s. However, this most recent rise may foreshadow a longer-run shift: a new age of scarcity, volatility, competition and conflict.

In the past century commodity prices fell while resources usage rose because there were such large, relatively easily accessible sources of supply. Finding equivalent sources of supply in the present century will be more difficult. New supplies of oil, gas, water and land will only be available in smaller pockets and in remote places more difficult and costly access. Meeting rising demand with current technologies would mean a 10 per cent increase in land under cultivation for food production, an additional 175 million to 220 million hectares of cropland, on top of the land lost to urbanisation and through environmental degradation. Demand for steel could be 80 per cent higher by 2030 to make possible the extraordinary growth of cities in the developing world. Supply would have to be expanded at unprecedented rates to meet this demand. Yet to achieve that would only invite further environmental risks and social pressures as mines and wells were dug deeper, into fragile landscapes and politically contested territories.

The affluent consumers of the West acquired their lifestyles in an unprecedented period, when we used massive amounts of resources at falling prices. In the next three decades several billion more people in the world will start earning enough to aspire to similar living standards. That demand will arrive as the world finds it increasingly difficult and costly to mobilise the resources needed to satisfy it using current technologies. As a result resources and commodities are likely to become more expensive. The only way out of this will be through unprecedented levels of innovation to create an economy designed to reward the husbandry of scarce resources rather than their wasteful exploitation.

In the developed world this would mean a wave of innovations to reduce waste and increase the efficiency with which resources are used.[20] In OECD countries, for example, one-third of fruit and vegetables bought by consumers are wasted, compared with just 5 per cent in sub-Saharan Africa which uses much more primitive systems for transporting and storing food. Reducing food waste at the point of consumption by 30 per cent would be the equivalent of 40 million hectares of cropland. Adjusting the temperature at which heaters and air-conditioning systems start working by just 2 degrees centigrade would reduce energy usage of heating and air-conditioning systems by 12 per cent. Retrofitting older buildings with improved insulation would reduce energy demand markedly, especially combined with a shift to more efficient lighting and household appliances. Encouraging denser urban development would reduce energy demand, especially for transport if more people relied on public transport systems, walking and cycling. Combined heat and power schemes, in which waste heat is recycled as an energy input into other processes, would transform the economics of energy-intensive industries and their neighbouring towns. If most cities emulated Phnom Penh, the capital of Vietnam, which loses just 5 per cent of the water in its pipes in leaks, then there would be no urban water crisis.[21]

These opportunities lie in the realm of the possible: reconfiguring existing systems to make them less profligate. Beyond them lie even more dramatic innovations, involving new technologies, products and systems to reduce resource usage, including: shifting most car transportation to hybrid electric vehicles with batteries powered by renewable sources of electricity generation; solar fuels, photosynthetic microorganisms such as algae that would use carbon dioxide and sunlight to make alternatives to oil; advanced, low-energy desalination technologies that use natural proteins to mimic the way nature removes salt from water; nanosteel restructured at micro level to make it stronger and lighter using tungsten;

soil management systems that use microbes to generate nutrients as an alternative to energy-intensive fertiliser; fuel cells that convert hydrogen to electricity at very low temperatures; new low-energy compressors for air-conditioning units and forms of glass that automatically adjust to the intensity of sunlight.

A Conceptual Crisis

Yet new technologies will not provide the answers unless they are matched by new thinking. As the philosopher Mary Midgley put it, we are facing not just an environmental crisis but a conceptual one, in the way in which we think of our relationship to natural systems.[22] Midgley argues the root of our troubles lies in the Enlightenment's separation of mind and body, man and nature, subject and object, which taught us to view nature as little more than a resource for our personal use: 'This has produced a huge harvest of knowledge … but it has made it very hard for people to even see how the parts might be put together.' The development economist Paul Collier, in his book *Plundered Planet*,[23] calls for an approach to natural systems that is neither instrumental nor naïvely romantic, which emphasises a sense of stewardship and responsibility. The systems of the future will have to work with the grain of the environment, rather than cutting through it, extracting from it, depositing waste into it. The systems of the future will have to be built on a renewed sense of our intimate, daily interdependence *with* nature rather than doing things to it, for our benefit.

Our industrial systems – the products that we make, buy and use – sit within larger natural systems on which they depend. Those natural systems provide: regenerative resources – forests, croplands, fisheries – which we can draw on so long as we do not overuse them; non-regenerative resources that we can only use once because they do not replenish themselves – oil, gas and coal; and waste services to digest, dilute and process the solid wastes we push out into the air, land and sea. Every factory needs to get its energy and raw material from somewhere and dispose of the water left behind in the process. All of that activity, beyond the production line, depends on natural systems and flows. The designers of the industrial systems that got us to where we are today did not have to think about the links between industrial and natural systems. They took it for granted that the earth would continue to provide coal and oil, fish and topsoil. Nor did they have to worry about the capacity of the earth, sea and atmosphere to absorb waste. Industrial systems were designed as if the environment could be taken for granted. The systems of the future will have to make this interdependence a central feature of their design. Peter Senge, the management thinker, in *The Necessary Revolution* is one of many calling for a new circular industrial model in which all forms of waste become inputs for other processes.[24] Indeed the innovations we will need in the future will take their design principles from natural systems, using waste from one process as the fuel for another, minimising transport costs by using local resources as far as possible, and using renewable energy wherever possible and very sparingly.

They will also require new levels of social coordination to manage our interdependence. That is why frugal solutions will be social as much as technological innovations.

Going Dutch

The Netherlands provides one example of the kind of social innovation that will be required to match the technological innovation we must invest in. The Netherlands is a densely populated, energy-intensive economy, in which almost all water levels have to be controlled as most of the land is below sea level. The Dutch have created the land they live on by putting in place astonishingly complex systems to prevent flooding, regulate land use and maintain an intricately connected set of dams, dykes, canals and pumping stations. The entire economy is hemmed in by its environmental vulnerability and only survives thanks to an extensive system of overlapping rules, regulations, political agreements and social norms to underpin reciprocity, known as the Polder model. The Netherlands manages this trick by being relatively ethnically homogenous, small, wealthy and well educated. In the next three decades we will have to pull off a trick like this on a global scale, with billions of people clamouring for a better standard of living, governments fearful of disappointing them, conflicts over resources barely contained, and the threat of global warming hanging over us, in often chaotic cities. It is not that there are too many people on the planet. Rosling is right: the problem is that the way we live together is so wasteful, profligate and destructive. We do not just need to innovate new technologies, products and services; we need to innovate cleaner, less wasteful, more attentive, egalitarian, convivial ways to live together.

None of this will be possible unless business understands and adapts to this new context, in which industrial systems have to work with and within natural systems. The kind of innovation we need will not just produce low-cost products but products that use fewer resources, more intelligently. Frugal innovation will need to be lean *and* clean. If not, then innovations to make products and services might simply increase demand and usage rather than reducing them. We would meet expanding demand but fatally breach our environmental limits.

5

The Swell

We face a conceptual crisis, not just an economic one. We do not need new growth so much as new ideas for how we should organise ourselves and, most importantly, for how we judge what it means to be economically successful. All of this provides a different context for innovation.

Innovation is most usually seen as a means of competition between companies seeking to differentiate themselves, getting ahead by creating new products, opening up new markets, deploying new technologies. The context for innovation is provided by other companies and the need to compete with them. This narrow perspective, focused on innovation as a facet of competition within industries and among companies, will still be vital but not enough in future. We also need to see innovation in a much wider context of, and as a response to, the more fundamental societal challenges we face: the constraints of competition over scarce resources in the context of climate change; the demands of the new price conscious middle class of the developing world; the sustained squeeze on the living standards of the middle classes of the developed world. The companies that will be successful in future will understand what this wider context means for competition and innovation within their industries. Successful innovators within industries will be those companies that respond to these wider challenges most creatively. We need solutions that come together to create a more inclusive, fairer, more stable and less destructive kind of capitalism, which will provide people with better ways to live. It is a tall order.

Reframing Innovation

The most powerful tool at our disposal is our growing, distributed and combined capacity for innovation, in its widest sense, to create new technologies, products, services, organisations and ways of living. Innovation is not just what comes out of large R & D labs. Innovation is how we rearrange the resources we have to get better results from them. The silicon in a computer is virtually worthless until it has minute patterns engraved on it. When that is delicately recombined with the other physical ingredients in a computer it becomes ten times more powerful than the same resources put together in a slightly different way. Innovation is all about finding these recipes, to combine and recombine the resources available to us in new and more effective ways. Invariably in business, innovation is not about inventing new technologies and products from scratch, but finding ways to create new combinations of existing ingredients that generate better solutions for people. When Henry Ford put together his innovation of mass manufacturing in the early years of the 20th century he drew on ideas and techniques he borrowed from the railroads (scheduling), meat packing (the moving conveyor belt) and the sewing machine industry (interchangeable parts). Ford was a maverick outsider who could see how a new combination could be brought into being. When that mass production process was honed and itself combined with mass sales and distribution it created a new business model. Steve Jobs was the outstanding commercial innovator of the later 20th century. Yet he too excelled at creating new combinations of existing ingredients: he called it joining up the dots. Many of the ingredients of the iPod, the iPhone and iPad were initially created by others, including early versions of the iTunes and the App Store. What Jobs did was to see how they could be brought together in the most commercially powerful and successful way.

The mystical power of innovation to conjure the new out of thin air has turned it into a kind of religion, providing hope for the future. The tenets of the faith are delivered in monthly instalments of *Wired* magazine and in the missionary zeal of Clayton Christensen, high-priest of disruptive innovation; the lessons in the art of design thinking from the design firm Ideo, the fount of Californian creativity, and the congregations at conferences such as TED and Poptech. The cathedrals of this faith are Apple stores, all soaring glass and illuminated by light, with artefacts laid out reverentially on the tables. Steve Jobs is this religion's patron saint and in common with most primitive religions this one won over the faithful with the demonstration of miracles being brought into the world: a computer so thin it could be slipped into an envelope; a tablet that could be controlled with the swipe of a finger; a tiny device that could contain an entire library of music. Innovation is a disciplined form of faith: to innovate you have to believe in something that does not yet exist. That is why innovation offers us a kind of redemptive hope for the future.

Yet, like many religions, innovation is prone to disappoint and even to become self-defeating. Too much innovation in a modern economy in which consumer markets are saturated is devoted to the proliferation of slightly different versions of existing products, to make them look and feel different, to persuade consumers they need to cast off what they already own to upgrade to something different. Too much innovation provides us with more, different products, rather than better solutions. That is because our current approach to innovation, framed almost entirely around the need for companies to compete with one another in existing markets, is too narrow.

It is too narrow in where it draws its ideas from: still predominantly the research labs of universities and large companies in the rich world. To tackle the challenges we face we will need a genuinely global, dispersed capacity for innovation, where new ideas are generated closer to where the solutions are needed. It is too narrow in the needs it addresses, primarily among the richer consumers of the developed world, too often neglecting the needs of the majority of poorer consumers. It is too narrow in the tools it uses. We need solutions that are avowedly low-tech and no-tech as well as high-tech; which embrace social innovation in health and education, alongside new technologies.

At its most basic, innovation is not just about new products, services and technologies but how we collectively learn to live more successful lives. The kind of innovation we need in the cramped, crushed context we face will enable us to live well but within our means, creating better solutions with fewer resources, in every sense. Innovation in the 21st century needs to be led by an ethic of elegant, effective frugality.

Frugal

To be frugal means to husband your resources carefully by thoughtfully making the most of everything you have and wasting as little as possible. Frugal is *paisa vasool*, good because it is enough, ample because it is sufficient. At first sight frugal innovation might seem like an oxymoron, an impossible, contradictory combination. Innovation is all about creating the new; frugality is about making do with what you have. Innovators break through constraints; the frugal live within them.

Frugal innovators use the constraints they operate under to their advantage, as a motive power for innovation. The often extreme and difficult conditions under which they operate become a spur to innovation, helping to generate new solutions. That is not to suggest that all innovation can or should be done on the cheap, nor that frugal innovators would not thrive with some additional resources. But being rich with resources, smart buildings, elaborate processes, hierarchies of knowledgeable people, can sometimes be an obstacle to innovation which has as its aim creating simpler, leaner solutions. When people have few resources it can confer on them advantages that the rich lack.

That is because it is easier to challenge conventional wisdom when you are clearly outside it, with no ingrained organisational cultures to battle or costly infrastructure to dismantle. Radical, disruptive innovation invariably starts in the margins serving demanding consumers who cannot afford high-end solutions. Extremity and crisis can breed urgency and ingenuity and provide focus. A lack of resources can feed a process of creative improvisation, making the most of what is already available rather than creating technologies and infrastructure from scratch. Not having a special environment in which to experiment and innovate can hold back fundamental research and radical thinking but it also encourages innovators to try things out in the real world, with real consumers. In the absence of a marketing and sales department, innovators have to rely more on their direct knowledge and interaction with real consumers, in real time. Doing without a team of specialist designers, with their bag of tricks, means that frugal innovators develop prototypes that are good enough without being perfect. Just as the vulnerable can be powerful and the introverted quietly persuasive, those operating under daunting constraints can come up with some of the most radical effective innovations.

Innovation thrives where hope and possibility meet constraints and obstacles, breeding first frustration and then ingenuity. As more people around the world find themselves at the meeting point of hope, constraint and frustration, so more will turn to forms of innovative self-help to find solutions.

Innovation invariably involves combining different ideas and technologies together to create a new recipe and solution. As a result innovation is also invariably a highly collaborative team activity. An innovation is only successful if it can answer several questions and risks: will the technology and the product work?; will consumers want it?; can it be made reliably at scale and can a business make money from it? An innovation can fail at each of these stages. Even if all the technical issues can be resolved and the product works, consumers might not see how they can incorporate it into their lives. Even if consumers want a product, it might not be possible for a company to make a profit providing it. Innovation involves resolving and overcoming technical, consumer and business risks. Resolving these different questions requires different skills and different types of people. That is why successful innovation is always a collaborative activity, often over quite a long time.

In the early stages of innovation there might be a premium on creativity, lateral thinking and openness to new ideas. As the work proceeds, other skills of project management, organisational design and business development become far more important. The innovation journey is often a protracted process that requires different people with different skills to play a role at different stages, working in teams that build up a sense of trust and momentum.

Leading innovation is about orchestrating that process of creative, collaborative combination. Sometimes those leaders can be charismatic, visionary, risk-takers. But equally they can be quietly spoken, do not grab the limelight and excel at getting the best from other people. Innovators have what psychologist Carol Dweck calls a 'growth mindset'.[25] In the face of uncertainty and constraints they see opportunities to create better outcomes for people even when they have fewer resources. People with a growth mindset are comfortable dealing with change, impatient with complacency and are natural problem-solvers. Their starting point is that people and organisations are capable of learning and growing all the time. The source of this growth mindset is that radical innovators invariably have a deep sense of vocation and mission: what they do is more than just a job.

The Makings of a Wave

Great ideas that change entire industries are like waves that start a long way off and gather momentum by drawing in contributions from many sources. Taking sole credit for a great idea is like a surfer taking credit for the wave. In the context we face we need to look for new waves of innovation. The best surfers understand the way the sea is changing, when and where the biggest and best waves are coming. That is the significance of the frugal innovators we profile in this book: like the best surfers, they have spotted the best waves to ride.

A swell of frugal innovation is gathering, fed from many sources: old ideas and new; large companies and smaller social enterprises; researchers in universities and grass-roots, barefoot entrepreneurs, from India and China but also California and Copenhagen.

Frugal innovation was first recognised in India as *jugaad*, a Hindi word meaning an improvised and resourceful solution that makes the most of what is available; patching things together using simple means. In their seminal book *Jugaad Innovation*,[26] Navi Radjou, Jaideep Prabhu and Simone Ahuja argue that frugal innovators reframe adversity as opportunity; learn to minimise the resources they need by piggybacking their solutions on existing infrastructures; enlist consumers as participants in creating markets and meeting their own needs; provide inventive financing models so consumers can buy just as much and no more than they need and create solutions that are good for their context. The improvisational creativity of *jugaad* innovation is not confined to India. In Brazil it is known as *gambiarra* and in Africa as *jua kali*. In the West it surfaces in the hacker ethic of do-it-yourself, do-it-together open source solutions and platforms for shared knowledge, designs and ideas, from Wikipedia to Linux and Thingiverse, the open source library of designs.

India has a prodigious movement of grass-roots, bottom-up innovators in the Gandhian tradition of production *by* the masses not for the masses. This movement embraces traditional, tacit forms of knowledge built up informally within communities over decades and spread by word of mouth, emulation and imitation. These are the kinds of solutions promoted by Anil Gupta's Honeybee Network in India,[27] with a mission to create 'more for less, for many' by connecting young innovators in college to local innovators developing new varieties of carrot and herbal remedies. Yet, as we will see, even in India grass-roots self-help and make-do is just one part of the frugal wave. Other contributions are coming from very big companies, some home-grown and others, like General Electric (GE), multinational in scope.

The Chinese equivalent of *jugaad* is known as *zizhu chuagxin* and it also shows up in *shanzai* companies, who got going by first copying designs from the West but then adapting them. The Chinese approach to innovation focuses on putting theoretical knowledge to work in practical ways, on the production line, rather than in the lab.[28] To the outside world this might look as if Chinese companies do not invest in innovation because they do not invest in research. In reality their approach is to focus on innovation as development in production rather than through research. A prime example is the development of the dense and interconnected cluster of Chinese motorcycle manufacturers and suppliers in Chongqing. Through this intense collaboration Chinese firms have learned how to design and build low-cost motorcycles far faster than their competitors. Production of motorcycles has risen from about 5 million a year in the mid-1990s to more than 20 million in 2010. The price of the average motorcycle has fallen from $700 to almost $200 and although the global market for motorcycles has expanded, the share taken by the long-time industry leaders – Honda, Yamaha and Suzuki – has fallen to less than 40 per cent. The Chongqing cluster is highly distributed, highly collaborative and lean all at the same time.[29]

The frugal wave is not, however, a purely local, grass-roots, or even a national phenomenon: it is decidedly cosmopolitan. In India and China, for example, many of the most powerful innovations have come from innovators who have a foot in both the developed and the developing world – they bridge both, bringing ideas from the West and applying them in new ways in their home markets. China excels at absorbing ideas from the West and reinterpreting them in a Chinese context. In both China and India, diasporas of knowledgeable and resourceful entrepreneurs and innovators are the most productive sources of new ideas. The best surfers of the frugal wave will be drawn from these diaspora networks.

China excels at absorbing ideas from the West and reinterpreting them in a Chinese context

Yet the roots of frugal innovation go wider and deeper than this current generation of innovators, solving the problems they see in front of them. Many draw on older ideas that are being brought back to life from the 1960s and 1970s in new form.

Perhaps the most important intellectual inspiration for the frugal wave is the alternative economist E. F. Schumacher, the author of *Small is Beautiful*,[30] published in 1973, which prefigured many of the ideas attracting attention today. Schumacher challenged orthodox economics and provided an imaginative synthesis of ideas to reframe the possible solutions. He argued scientific and technological innovation had become a self-interested and self-fulfilling system: 'In his excitement over the unfolding of his scientific and technical power modern man has built a system of production that ravishes nature and a type of society that mutilates man.' *Small is Beautiful* is a manifesto for frugal innovation. Schumacher argued that what we need from scientists and technologists are 'methods and equipment which are cheap enough so they are accessible to virtually everyone; suitable for small scale application and compatible with man's need for creativity'. These intermediate, useful, simple, down-to-earth technologies would feed a democratic, dispersed creativity. New forms of production would need to be matched, however, by new lifestyles that saw value more in relationships and the quality of experience we had than in the pleasure of ownership of objects. Schumacher was suspicious of centralised, monolithic, large-scale solutions, which put power in the hands of elites and put everyone's eggs in a single basket of technologies. Instead he argued for solutions that were appropriate to their setting and which encouraged a mass of smaller-scale experiments and adaptations. (The real argument of *Small is Beautiful* is that appropriate scale and proportion for the context is better. But 'Appropriate for the Context' is not a great title.) The best organisations, Schumacher argued, were like a group of balloons, held together but each with its own buoyancy, shape, colour and lift. Schumacher was one of the first to see the connections between how capitalism treated people and how it treats the environment. He argued the modern industrial economy was engaged in a battle for control over natural resources which, if we won, we would nevertheless find ourselves on the losing side.

Many others are joining the wave Schumacher inspired. Designers and engineers are adding their formal, professional knowledge to these grass-roots efforts, from Santa Clara University's frugal design lab, to Stanford's programme of entrepreneurial design for extreme environments to Cambridge University's engineering programme for socially responsible design. A new wave of young designers, inspired by Victor Papanek's 1971 polemic *Design for the Real World*,[31] are turning their backs on designing for richer consumers in favour of meeting unmistakable basic social needs. As design commentator Barbara Bloemink put it in the catalogue to the Smithsonian exhibition *Design for the Other 90%*: 'These designers recognize that by actively understanding the available resources, tools, desires and immediate needs of their potential users – how they live and work – they can design simple, functional and potentially open source objects and systems that will enable the users to become more empowered, self-supporting entrepreneurs in their own right.'[32] Perhaps the foremost exponent of this art, Paul Polak, founder of International Development Enterprises, argues the key is to design products and systems that are affordable, light, portable and modular, so they can expand, contract and move as needed.[33] Fixed, heavy, complex systems do not work in the developing world. Polak argues that going back to earlier, cheaper versions of a technology that were prematurely discarded, is often the best way to find these solutions. Effective solutions need to be designed with the communities who will use them and that favours solutions which are relatively familiar and easy to adopt. This social design movement is starting to make itself felt in many different areas, from Architecture for Humanity, to Archeworks, an alternative design school in Chicago, to the Massachusetts Institute of Technology's D-Lab, under the leadership of visionary engineer Amy Smith, another surfer.

These designers are working in tandem with social entrepreneurs who are seeking economically viable, market-based solutions to pressing social needs. Relying on either charity or government is potentially demeaning and risky. A far more secure and reliable way to meet people's needs is to serve them as consumers with decent products they can afford. These social entrepreneurs are being backed by a growing band of social impact investors, led by the Acumen Fund based in New York and the Gates Foundation, who are seeking out innovative solutions, often in partnership with government aid agencies.[34] Many of these entrepreneurs were inspired by C. K. Prahalad's groundbreaking work, *The Fortune at the Bottom of the Pyramid*,[35] written at the beginning of the 21st century, which was the first serious attempt to reframe the challenge of meeting the needs of the poor as a market opportunity to create affordable solutions. One of Prahalad's early collaborators, Stuart Hart, now at the Johnson School of Management at Cornell University, takes this a step further by arguing that these 'bottom-of-the-pyramid' markets are an opportunity for disruptive, low-cost, green innovation, which could percolate back into the richer markets of the developed world. Hart echoes Schumacher in arguing for solutions that are 'small in scale, distributed in character and almost always disruptive to established big organisations'.[36]

Hart's focus on how these marginal markets could be the breeding ground for new sustainable technologies forms a bridge to another group of innovators seeking an alternative to linear, resource-intensive and wasteful industrial systems. Amory and Hunter Lovins' in *Natural Capitalism* set out the case for closed-loop, circular systems, which recycle and reuse their own waste.[37] Paul Hawken, in *The Ecology of Commerce* published in 1993, put the challenge and the opportunity this way: 'To create an enduring society we will need a system of commerce and production where each and every act is inherently sustainable and restorative.'[38] Whereas linear, industrial systems are based on a process of take-make-dispose-and-waste, restorative capitalism would have to work with the ebbs and flows of energy from the sun and plants. Hawken warned: 'Having expropriated resources from the natural world in order to fuel a transient period of materialistic freedom, we must now restore those resources and accept the limits and discipline inherent in that relationship. Until business accepts this responsibility, it will continue to be maladaptive and predatory.'

Running through all of this is not just a new account of how we use resources and make things, but how we consume. New aspirational lifestyles would be needed to bring new production systems to life. One ingredient of this is a new respect for the role of consumers as partners in innovation and sometimes the originators of it. Consumers are not always best placed to understand their own needs but often some of them are, especially when they face extreme and difficult circumstances. Consumer-innovators are by necessity frugal, they have to experiment in the real world, at low cost, and adapt what is already available rather than starting from scratch.

These different innovators and ideas, working in different contexts, are starting to come together in a series of building waves that will bring with them rounds of innovation linking funders, designers, grass-roots innovators, consumers, social entrepreneurs and big business. Despite coming from very different starting points, this nascent movement shares common principles.

The Dutch commentators Michiel Schwarz and Joost Elffers have tried to put a name to this nascent movement, which they call *Sustainism*, a new worldview of how to live which makes the most of both our interconnections and our constraints. Our growing connections, with one another and with nature, are hugely creative and productive. Connections can breed ideas, meaning and culture. But our connections to one another and our environment also create constraints and place limits on our freedom to act. Understanding the creative nature of constraints will be vital to future innovation, they argue, as will knowing that how to make things last is as important as being able to make something new.

Schumacher elegantly articulated the shared principles underlying this movement more than 40 years ago. He advocated solutions that were: conducive to decentralisation; appropriate technologies to their setting and compatible with the laws of ecology; gentle in their use of scarce resources and designed to serve people rather than making people servants of systems. Experiments that start in what appear to be margins can remake mass, mainstream markets. The frugal innovations we will need in the decades to come will surf this mounting wave of ideas. At their core they will have four common design principles. They will be: *lean* to minimise waste; *simple*, so they are easy to use in many different settings; *social* to create shared solutions and experiences, which bring people together and reduce costs; *clean*, by recycling, restoring and renewing what we have already. Those principles should be at the core of frugal innovation and they are the focus of the next four chapters.

chapter **6**

Lean

Bangalore's Hosur Road is one of the best places to visit to understand where frugal innovation will come from. On a Monday morning it is a snaking, obstinate long traffic jam enveloped in dust as thousands of people mill around the near stationary cars visiting roadside restaurants, stalls, shacks and temples. Everything is for sale on the Hosur Road, from sheets of steel and earth-moving equipment to geneticists and heart operations. Next to shacks covered in blue plastic are buildings designed for US-style business parks. Places such as this – hot, crowded, dirty, turbulent, needy – will be the breeding grounds for innovations that change our world, just as much as the universities and R & D centres of the US and Europe. For Hosur Road brings together three critical ingredients for really radical innovation, of the kind that can remake industries and even ways of life: need, knowledge and ingenuity. There is no need for market research. The pressing scale of the need that young, poor people have for better solutions – places to live, forms of transport, healthcare – is right in front of you. Bangalore has attracted an eclectic bunch of people, with knowledge gleaned from all over the world, from industry as well as academia and science. When those people use the advantages of their marginal location – isolated from the great centres of healthcare research – to the full then they can rewrite conventional wisdom. That is exactly what

Devi Shetty has done for healthcare, making himself perhaps the world's most famous frugal innovator in the process.

Shetty got the work in Bangalore because barriers to entry in science are falling fast. Knowledge and ideas are emerging from many more sources. Developing nations can build up clusters of world-class knowledge, even while the rest of the economy remains backward and much of the population lives in dire poverty. It is easier to connect to these pools of knowledge, to attract talent from them or send work to them, than ever before. Once-closed, controlled and largely national approaches to innovation are becoming more networked, open and collaborative. Investment in research and innovation will shift around the world in search of the best brains and the solutions they are creating. It will become more distributed. Parts of the innovation process will be parcelled up. That in turn will expand our collective capacity for innovation: we will be able to propose, test, prototype, develop at lower cost and greater speed. These new ideas and solutions are being created by new people in new places. The people are often mobile, partly Western-educated, fluent in English, cosmopolitan in outlook, easy to deal with, highly driven and yet locally rooted, often by family ties. These boundary-crossers are circular migrants, moving back and forth between places like Bangalore and Silicon Valley. When all that brainpower starts to meet new challenges, faced by people with only meagre resources, then it will start to develop new low-cost solutions. That is what Devi Shetty has done, without planning to.

Shetty was born in Karnataka, Bangalore's home state, and trained locally before going to the UK to study at Guy's Hospital in London. He returned to India to work in a hospital that treated Mother Teresa. Shetty was taken aback when she told him that God had put him on earth to cure children sick with heart disease. Shetty took up her challenge but has done so with a relentless drive to apply modern production methods to serve the poorest people. Shetty is both cosmopolitan and rooted, a doctor inspired by a moral mission who uses tools honed by Toyota and Walmart to achieve social ends.

Dubbed the Henry Ford of heart surgery, Shetty has single-mindedly sought the best way to do open-heart surgery, on an industrial scale. The result is that his family-owned hospital chain Narayana Hrudayalaya (NH) now does hundreds of basic heart operations each month, for anything between $2,000 and $5,000 per operation. Not only is this much cheaper than similar operations in the US, which can cost from $20,000 to $100,000, but the NH group also makes higher profit margins and delivers higher quality. Shetty has created a business that makes money, while offering its services at a fraction of the price of its peers and serving a poor population, many of whom cannot afford the full price.

One part of his recipe is the scale at which NH works. Shetty is no Schumacher: for heart bypass operations, big is beautiful. Founded in 2001 the initial hospital had 1,000 beds. This has evolved to form the core of an industrial complex, almost like its own city, with more than 5,000 beds. Alongside the original heart hospital, a world-class cancer centre has been built with the support of Biocon, one of the first biotech companies to set up shop on the Hosur Road, as well as an eye hospital, and centres for orthopaedics and neuroscience. Shetty has ambitious plans for hospitals with more than 25,000 beds across India. Already NH is operating in 14 Indian cities. These large volumes have helped to spread fixed costs over a much larger population. NH uses its buying power to get supplies direct from their manufacturers at lower unit prices.[39]

The volume has also brought lots of data that makes it possible to compare the performance of doctors, who are measured on the time they take per operation, the number of stitches they use and the amount of blood used in transfusions. There is no room for waste. NH relentlessly applies the unforgiving disciplines of lean manufacturing and total quality management to drive continual, incremental improvements in performance. Like a Japanese car factory, the NH heart hospital is modelled on a continual flow. About 24 open heart operations are conducted daily and 35 bypass operations, more than eight times the Indian average.

That level of efficiency only comes from the patients being managed as a seamless flow through the theatres, with the surgeons focused only on what they do best – operating – and leaving other staff to fill in the paperwork, to prepare the patients and take them to post-operative care. It is a team effort: NH's efficiency depends on a myriad of minor innovations, from across all members of the medical teams.

NH can only have such an efficient process, however, and meet its social mission to help those in greatest need by innovating as a business: that is, in how it makes money. The business model is designed to make the most of the self-motivation doctors have to do a better job. Doctors are paid a fixed salary, well below US levels. That means if a doctor does more treatments, the average cost falls. In the US doctors are paid per activity, therefore more operations mean more costs. NH has innovated on the customer side as well, to ensure it has a flow of patients on the scale needed to keep it operating at full capacity. With the government's support it has developed a micro-insurance system that costs as little as 22 cents a month for a poorer patient to gain basic cover. The hospital charges people according to their ability to pay. Those who can, including many hundreds each year from outside India, pay a full price, with their own air-conditioned room. Their fees subsidise poorer patients who cannot afford to pay and who are looked after in much more basic facilities. About 60 patients are treated for free each day. The mix is adjusted daily to make sure the hospital continues to make money and meets its social mission. Shetty gets a text stating the hospital's financial position at the end of each day. The social mission helps to motivate the doctors to do a better job regardless of how much they are paid. NH is both lean and social, money making and a moral crusade.

It is also only just getting going. Little more than a decade old, it is already one of the most innovative hospitals in the world. NH is starting to disperse its services away from Bangalore. Since 2002 it has offered 21,000 telemedicine consultations, mainly by using a Skype service installed on surgeons' laptops. (Skype itself is a good example of a frugal innovation: by piggybacking on the Internet it has created a low-cost, multipurpose, good enough global communications system. So this is a frugal innovator,

NH, using another frugal innovation, Skype, to create a new solution: distributed healthcare.) NH runs 17 local coronary care centres, where people can be treated before having to visit a consultant. Shetty is dispersing more than 5,000 dialysis machines across India to create a national kidney care service.

NH started life almost as a lean, high-volume factory system for heart operations done on a vast scale in a centralised facility; it is becoming, in addition, more dispersed and networked and lean, while offering localised solutions. That recipe will be the most interesting new model for services in the future: a combination of centralised and decentralised, networked and lean production.

Lean and Networked

Pedro Yrigoyen does not look like a medical revolutionary, for a good reason. His background is in telemarketing. Most of the medical profession regard him as a dangerous heretic. He looks more like an ageing rock star than a doctor: wearing jeans, driving a shiny Range Rover with bulletproof doors and blacked-out windows, he wears his shirts out and his long black hair slicked back. Yet Yrigoyen is promoting a challenge to the established orthodoxy that better health depends on employing more doctors and building more hospitals and clinics. He has devised a new low-cost way of providing high-quality primary healthcare to underserved and poor populations.

The focal point for Yrigoyen's revolution is a drab office on the upper floors of a block in a busy inner suburb of Mexico City, where a team of 20 paramedics, dressed in starched white coats, sit in cubicles waiting to answer phones. Yrigoyen cut his teeth running call centres: his system makes sure each call is answered within three seconds. The medics are fully trained but supported by computer systems loaded with protocols for diagnosing conditions that have been gathered from some of the best hospitals in the world. If necessary they can refer a call to a specialist doctor. This little call centre is the heart of a system, MedicallHome, which provides a bare-bones primary healthcare system for about 1 million Mexican households for just $5 a month. Almost by accident, because he lacked resources and came from outside the healthcare industry, Pedro Yrigoyen has invented a new, low-cost way to provide not just a frugal health system.

Mexico spends about 6.5 per cent of its GDP on healthcare, well below the average for most rich countries. As a result, access to doctors and nurses is limited, especially in poorer and rural areas. Mexico has 1.5 doctors per 1,000 people compared with 2.9 among OECD countries, and 2 nurses per 1,000 people compared with 8 in the OECD. About 54 per cent of health spending is accounted for by government services, which are nominally free. However, because these services are thinly spread, the cost of accessing them is very high, especially for people in rural areas, who have to travel a long way to see a doctor only to find they have to join a long queue. In common with many public services in the developing world, healthcare in Mexico is free in name only: patients have to pay a range of additional charges to get treatments once they have seen the doctor.

The public sector's failings have created a space in which a thriving low-cost private sector alternative has grown. Private health accounts for 46 per cent of healthcare spending in Mexico and about 94 per cent of health expenses are paid by patients out of their own pockets. For poor people the consequence is that healthcare expenses are often catastrophically high. They need a low-cost way to access decent healthcare. Yet the market is highly fragmented and variable.

That was not the challenge that Yrigoyen set out to take on. He was thinking in much more basic terms. In the mid-1990s his main business was running premium rate phone lines, 1-900 numbers, in which people paid a higher rate fee to listen to other people talking, often about sex. He was trying to expand the business by looking for other topics people would pay extra to talk about and hit on health as a possible market. So he set up a 1-900 number and sat a doctor in front of a phone to talk to the people who called. The business was not a success. They almost closed down twice. But just as they were contemplating closing, the mobile phone revolution started to sweep through Mexico. People who were struggling to pay for food, housing and transport, found the resources to buy a mobile phone. Pedro launched a health service for mobile phone users: for $5 a month, added to their phone bill, they would have 24/7 access to a medical doctor over a phone, to give them the best advice based on the procedures of the best hospitals in the world. Subscriptions for MedicallHome are sold door-to-door and through call centres. It is really a service for mothers who want peace of mind about their family. A million Mexican households are signed up to the service that covers almost 5 million people.

The service saves people money in several ways through lean thinking. Most of the issues – 62 per cent – are resolved first time, over the phone, which means that patients do not have to visit a doctor, which would cost at least $30 and involve missing a day's work. If the telephone doctor recommends the patient visit a doctor in person, have a blood test or take a treatment, then MedicallHome connects them to one of its network of 6,000 accredited doctors or 3,000 healthcare providers, in 233 cities. As MedicallHome refers patients in large numbers, it negotiates discounts for them ranging from 5 to 50 per cent. MedicallHome is becoming a market place: patients will get discounts; providers will get referrals. MedicallHome provides a basic primary healthcare service for 5 million people with just 90 doctors and paramedics. A traditional healthcare system would require 1,000 doctors in expensive dedicated facilities to service 5 million people. Not surprisingly MedicallHome's main investor is Carlos Slim, Mexico's richest man and the owner of Latin America's largest mobile phone group, which takes a large chunk of the service's revenues.

MedicallHome has come up with a radical, frugal innovation – an ultra low-cost primary healthcare system – but only because it made its lack of resources work for it: using its marginal position to dispense with orthodox thinking; riding the rising tide of mobile networks and resisting conventional wisdom. As mobile networks spread across Latin America so did MedicallHome's solution, initially to Colombia, Ecuador and Peru. Lean, networked self-help solutions of this kind are starting to emerge all over the developing world as the mobile phone spreads. Perhaps the most famous is M-Pesa, the Kenyan mobile banking system, which now has 17 million registered users and allows participants to transfer money without going through a bank, using text messages. The money can be collected from local retailers who act as M-Pesa's physical distribution network. M-Pesa has created a banking system without needing ATM machines or a large physical network of its own.

The Origins of Lean

Lean thinking is central to frugal innovation and to understand lean thinking we have to go back to Japan, after the end of the Second World War – a society in crisis, without natural resources, a population near starvation – where in conditions of extreme austerity, making a little from a lot became a national way of life.

There is a good reason why the world's most powerful car companies did not spot the revolution in production techniques that would sweep through the industry from the 1970s. That revolution – lean production – started as most radical innovations do, in a backwater, cut off from the mainstream. Moreover it was a backwater occupied by a minnow that at the time produced a few thousand cars a year, little more than a craft producer compared with Detroit where millions of cars are rolled off the production lines. Yet the rules of the industry were about to be remade not by the strongest companies but by one of the weakest, Toyota, the fledgling and fragile Japanese car company that in 1949 was almost on its last legs. Even if the big car companies had managed to identify Toyota as a disruptive innovator, they would not have been able to make sense of what it was up to because seen from the vantage point of the conventional wisdom of mass production it looked chaotic and crazy. Yet in Toyota's position, doing something mad made perfect sense.

Toyota did not have a grand plan to create a new way to make cars at low cost, at high quality and with minimal waste. Instead its engineers were intent on solving a host of problems that beset the company. Although these innovations became known as lean production, for the first ten years of their life, they had no name.

Toyota started life among the farmers of Nagoya and made its name as a brand of textile machines. It went into vehicle production only in the

1930s and it was not a success. By 1949, with the Japanese economy still ravaged by the after-effects of war and the country under US occupation, Toyota suffered a deep slump in sales. A proposal to cut the workforce by 25 per cent provoked a lengthy strike that led to the resignation of the president Kiichiro Toyoda. At that point, after 13 years in the car business, Toyota had made just 2,685 cars.[40] At the time Ford Motor Company's River Rouge plant was producing 7 million a year. Yet that crisis was the turning point in the company's fortunes because it propelled Toyota to find a novel solution to the tight constraints it was working under and that solution would allow them to remake the industry.

Roughly speaking there were just two ways to make cars. The first was craft production in which highly skilled craftsmen working with general-purpose tools made a bespoke product for an elite of customers. This is how the car industry started, with thousands of producers making just a handful of cars for a few consumers. Detroit emerged as the centre of the 20th-century car industry because the companies that made it their home, Ford and General Motors, adopted a different approach: mass manufacturing. Ford made millions of cars, in a few models, employing semi-skilled workers organised in a division of labour to operate expensive, heavy-duty machinery that was dedicated to repeating the same task over and over again. The machines were expensive, so they had to be run at full capacity, for as many hours as possible, doing the same job. Delays could not be tolerated. So often mistakes were passed on down the line, to be corrected or ignored later, just to keep the line moving. Poor quality was a price the company was prepared to pay for high volumes. Large buffer stocks of inventory were needed just in case the production line ran short. It was a powerful but inflexible system, overseen by layers of supervisors, engineers and managers. Toyota could not afford this approach: it had neither the capital nor the level of production and demand to make it work. The extremity of its position meant it had to think afresh. That is where Taiichi Ohno comes in.

Ohno, Toyota's engineering director, faced severe constraints that in turn spurred him to radical innovation. Toyota was broke; he had a very limited capital budget; the company made cars in very small batches so he could not afford fixed machines that were dedicated to a single task. Machines would have to be interchanged and adapted to undertake several different tasks as they made different models. That meant they needed a workforce that was skilled, committed and flexible enough to switch around the machines as needed. On mass manufacturing lines in the US it took at least a day of lost production to switch one machine for another. Within a year, Ohno and his team had reduced to three minutes the time it took to change one machine for another so they could switch models. They then found that if they applied the same work ethic to other aspects of production, costs would fall, waste would be eliminated and quality would improve. They had found a new recipe for being efficient, despite not producing in high volumes: lean production.

Toyota could not afford the profligacy of mass manufacturing that tolerated high levels of waste and poor quality. Ohno's enemy was *muda*, waste in all its forms, which he defined as human activities that absorb resources without creating any value. Instead of mistakes that require correction, Ohno wanted workers to get it right first time. He saw no reason to have expensive stocks of inventory in case something went wrong and from that emerged the idea of just-in-time production: components arriving only as they were needed on the line. That eliminated costly buffer stocks of inventory; the plant has just as much as it needs and no more – an ample sufficiency you might say.

Lean production only works by reimagining the process of making a product or delivering a service.[41] Workers are encouraged to work in teams to exercise direct and shared responsibility to solve quality problems as they arise, stopping the production line if necessary. As James Womack and Daniel Jones put it in their seminal account of the rise of lean production, *The Machine that Changed the World*: 'The truly lean plant has two key organisational features. It transfers the maximum number of tasks and responsibilities to those works actually adding value to the car on the line, and it has in place a system for detecting defects that quickly traces every problem, once discovered, to its ultimate cause.'

That requires teamwork which goes well beyond the plant to incorporate the suppliers who have to work as part of the team to deliver small batches of components several times a day, as and when they are needed. All this demands widespread sharing of information on the state of production, so everyone can see what will be needed and when. Lean production systems thrive on open, shared information. Everyone has to take responsibility, so everyone needs to know what is going on. Lean production got started in car plants but the fundamental unit in a lean system is the team or even the community of workers, suppliers and customers, sharing information about what needs to be produced and when. To run a lean factory, hospital, school or bank, an organisation has to orchestrate not just what happens inside the organisation but its network of suppliers and how it recruits its customers, so work flows in an orderly fashion. As Womack and Jones define it: 'Lean thinking is *lean* because it provides a way to do more and more with less and less, less human effort, less equipment, less time, less space – while coming closer and closer to providing customers with exactly what they want.' Lean production is both highly systematic and highly relational; it depends on relentless measurement to improve performance but also on committed teamwork among capable people who trust one another.

The Toyota Production System is an inspirational example of frugal innovation. Toyota responded to the extreme constraints it was working under and made the most of its marginal position as a minor producer to turn conventional wisdom inside out. In the process it developed a lean approach to making cars, the principles of which are now being applied to health, education, banking, construction and food distribution. Like Toyota those innovators will not be found in the mainstream but under the radar in the overlooked margins, such as the Lebanon.

The Lean School

The Sabis group is doing for education what NH is doing for heart surgery: it is the closest anyone has yet come to creating a Toyota production system for learning. Like NH the Sabis group started in an unlikely place: a small Christian school for girls on Mount Lebanon in the late 19th century.[42] For most of its life, the village school struggled to survive: it lived through the collapse of the empires and two world wars. What turned Sabis into a radical innovator was the most extreme condition imaginable: the onset of Lebanon's bloody civil war in 1975, the subsequent Israeli invasion in 1982, followed by Syrian occupation. The civil war had brought the original school to its knees; it was on the verge of bankruptcy. The school's salvation was international expansion. Lebanese who fled the country and found refuge in Gulf States wanted a school they could trust. In responding to their demand Sabis realised that to expand beyond its home it would need a reliable system, to translate its home-grown approach to new sites. Sabis's remarkable lean education system was born in the midst of crisis. It now applies this approach across a chain of 12 schools from the Middle East, to the UK, Europe and the US. That system could eventually inspire solutions that provide education to millions of children at very low cost. It is lean to its core and this is how it works.

Sabis works back from the final exams that students have to do – the International Baccalaureate or A levels – to establish what key concepts children need to learn at each stage of their education. Each subject is broken down into a set of essential and non-essential concepts. In maths for Grade 4, for example, there might be 300 concepts that need to be covered in a year. Those concepts are then organised into a timely flow, like components on a production line, which children have to learn and teachers teach. To check on progress each week, in every subject, children in every Sabis school complete a largely automated test to show what they have learned. Sabis has a central bank of almost 1 million questions it has trialled to test student capability. The questions themselves are graded bronze to platinum according to how well they perform in highlighting where students are strong and where weak. The results of the tests, usually done on computers, are relayed to the teachers and to the Sabis group headquarters[42] so they can quickly identify who needs extra help mastering the concepts they learned that week and which teachers are doing the best job. Like a Toyota production line, problems are not allowed to build up; they have to be fixed there and then. Children are not allowed to fall behind. These tests, combined with teacher assessments, provide the school with reams of data about each child, in each subject and each class, and also about their teachers. In an average school in the UK, for example, a parent might get a report once a term with a brief paragraph from each subject teacher combined with an overall mark of performance. At a Sabis school the file on how a Grade 7 child is doing at mathematics might run to 102 pages. Each concept learned will have a quality mark attached to it, showing how thoroughly it was learned. The data also allow Sabis to check on the quality of teachers. Discrepancies in performance quickly show up. Academic teams, like quality circles, work with teachers to improve the scores their children get.

Yet Sabis does not just rely on technology to do a good job. Like Toyota, its lean systems depend on the commitment of the entire school community. It is a social solution, not just a technological one. The most striking aspect of this is how much teaching the students do for one another.

Skilled teachers – like surgeons in an operating theatre – are the scarcest resources in a school. Sabis makes sure teachers are only focused on teaching; all administrative chores and paperwork are handled by support staff. However, even Sabis finds it hard to recruit teachers with the quality it needs in all the places where it operates. So to supplement its teachers' efforts children are encouraged to take on some teaching responsibilities. Students who finish a task fast because they understand it are encouraged to help those who are lagging behind. Taking on a teaching role, explaining difficult concepts, helps to embed their own learning. Instead of sitting around getting bored while the rest of the class catches up, they contribute to the learning of other students. Each class in a Sabis school will have a couple of shadow teachers – pupils – who will take over when a teacher is absent. As a result Sabis schools do without supply teachers, who are often regarded as fair game by children. If a Sabis teacher is absent then the shadow teachers step in and they are expected to teach properly, taking on new concepts, rather than simply trying to hold the fort. Students take responsibility for running large parts of the school, from discipline to sports, through the Student Life organisation of which all are members. The more the children can be self-governing, the less time teachers have to spend on non-teaching activities. The most precious, costly resource – the teachers – is focused on what it does best: teaching.

Although Sabis is rigorous and unrelenting, it tries to avoid a culture of competition, instead emphasising that classes move forward together, cooperatively. Students are not ranked. As Ralph Bistany, one of its co-founders, explained: 'One of the results of rankings is that one kid has an interest in somebody else's failure. It should not be you or me, but you and me. When people cooperate wealth increases and everybody has more.'

The opportunities for lean and frugal innovation in education are so large because the waste of talent is so immense. That is propelling innovators and social entrepreneurs all over the developing world to find better, lower-cost ways to educate millions of people on only very modest incomes at high quality.

Hundreds of millions of families send their children to school every day with the hope that education will change their lives for the better. Education plays a vital role in economic development, by providing skills and knowledge to make the economy more productive. Many families see in education qualifications that will lead their children to better jobs and higher incomes. Education should be generative: it should bring multiple benefits to people and over a very long time. Education offers people the hope that their place in society will not be fixed by where they were born. Yet, as it stands, schools deliver an education in frustration.

For all the hope that it excites, schooling can be rigid and bureaucratic, conservative and inflexible, resistant to new ideas and difficult to reform. That unwillingness to adapt means that education, far from delivering social mobility, can entrench social inequality. Inflexible, impersonal and rigid systems of poor quality, rote learning, are more likely to reinforce rather than break through inequalities of class, caste and gender. These failings are wasting talent on an epic scale.

Enrolments in school have risen fast in the last two decades. Worldwide, the number of children of primary school age who were out of school dropped from 103 million in 1999 to 73 million in 2006. Between 1995 and 2008 gross secondary school enrolment ratios in sub-Saharan Africa rose from 25 per cent to 34 per cent, in South Asia they rose from 44 per cent to 51 per cent and in East Asia from 64 per cent to 74 per cent. Yet too few of these children are learning anything useful. The key to improving the quality of traditional schools is the recruitment, training, motivation and management of teachers. The 2002 and 2006 World Absenteeism Survey, conducted by the World Bank, found that public school teachers in countries such as Bangladesh, Ecuador, Indonesia and Peru miss one day in five. These rigid, inflexible, impersonal systems then lead to waste on a huge scale in the form of drop-outs and exam failures. A survey by Pratham, India's leading educational non-governmental organisation (NGO), found that only 35 per cent of children in the 6th grade could read a story and only 30 per cent could do maths calculations designed for children in the 2nd grade. In West Bengal, for example, only 17 of 100 students starting primary education will reach their school leaving exams. By the beginning of the 20th century all Brazilian children had a place at school. The illiteracy rate among 14-year-olds has fallen to 2.5 per cent. Girls had access to education on the same basis as boys. Yet one study found that half the resources of Brazilian education are spent on pupils repeating grades.

Parents and communities are already responding to the crisis in public education in the developing world by creating solutions that seem impossible: lean, local, low-cost private schools for the poor. In the rich world, private schools are for the rich. In the developing world, low-cost private schools are spreading like wildfire, as parents search for better ways to educate their children when state systems let them down. A quarter of children in rural areas of Pakistan go to low-cost private primary schools. In Karachi 50 per cent of children are educated by the private sector. In the poorer areas of Lagos, Nigeria, 75 per cent of children are attending low-cost, often unregistered private schools. In the district of Ga in Ghana, which has about 500,000 inhabitants, three-quarters of whom live below the poverty line, 75 per cent of the schools are low-cost private schools.

In the Indian city of Hyderabad one survey of 19 registered slums found that 65 per cent of children enrolled in school were in low-cost private schools.[43] Geeta Gandhi Kingdon, an Oxford University expert on education policy in the developing world, estimates that 96 per cent of the increased enrolments in Indian primary schools between 1993 and 2000 were in often ramshackle private schools.[44] Teachers in private schools are paid a fifth of the wages their colleagues in the state sector receive, and yet generally produce better results. The difference is that school owners make sure the teachers turn up every day and teach.

The quality of low-cost private schools varies enormously. Few have the scale and sophistication of Sabis. Some are run by charlatans. Yet many deliver amazing value for money with a simple recipe. In Pakistan one study suggested that children at comparable government schools would need another two years' education to catch up with their counterparts at low-cost private schools, where teachers are less experienced, younger and less qualified. These schools are also more likely to cater for girls, because they are local and staffed mainly by women from the local community. Low-cost private schools are lean by instinct: they operate on tight margins. In Pakistan, for example, estimates suggest that it costs about PKR 1,200 per month, about $12, to run a class and parents pay about PKR120–230 a month ($1.20–2.40) in fees. The average school makes a profit of perhaps PKR 14,000 a year, about $142. Low-cost private schools are lean, localised, small-scale, distributed solutions, which make education of reasonable quality accessible even to the poorest households.

A new wave of entrepreneurs is entering this field to take some of these solutions to scale. The most impressive to date include the Citizens Foundation in Pakistan, a non-profit organisation, funded by citizen donations, which has built close to 1,000 low-cost schools in poor areas. In Africa, PEAS (Promoting Equality in African Schools) is running a clutch of schools in Uganda and Rwanda; the Omega chain is working in Ghana, and perhaps most impressive of all is the phenomenal growth of the Bridge International Academy network in Kenya, which by 2013 was running 600 schools, charging parents $4.50 a month for a high-quality primary education. Each of these is an exemplary case of frugal innovation: they deliver better results than the cumbersome, costly bureaucratic state systems while employing a fraction of the resources of equivalent public schools.

But for Ralph Bistany the lean school is just a step towards what he believes should be the future of education in the developing world: the ultra low-cost, teacherless school.

Bistany argues that children can learn as effectively from games, puzzles and texts on computers as they can by listening to a teacher explaining something at the front of a class. Children could learn as much listening to a teacher present through a live video link. Almost all of the tests that Sabis administers are delivered by computer. Much of the additional interactive teaching in a class setting can be done, peer to peer, in groups, led by shadow teachers. Sabis schools have strict discipline, but much of it is maintained by the Student Life organisation. With these components in place – computer-aided learning and testing, peer-to-peer learning and teaching, strong student self-governance and discipline – it should be possible for children to learn, en masse, without the need for an army of teachers to organise the process. Toyota eliminates waste, raises productivity, cuts costs and improves quality by passing as much responsibility as it can to people directly involved in production, where value is created. Similarly Ralph Bistany wants schools in the poorest areas to be able to concentrate as much of their meagre resources as they can on how children learn, often by enabling them to learn from one another and through computers, rather than relying on teachers, who in turn need management and support.

This idea of the ultra lean, teacherless, self-governing, computer-based school might seem fanciful and far-fetched to Western ears, but in the developing world this kind of approach is just straightforward problem-solving: the mad makes sense. Good teachers are hard to come by at the best of times, especially in subjects such as physics and mathematics. Recruiting teachers to work in slum schools is hard; to persuade them to work in distant rural schools even harder. To meet demand from young, growing populations the poorest countries will need to recruit and train millions of new teachers. The scale of the task is daunting. In

China, India, Indonesia and Nigeria alone, 10 million more teachers will be needed to bring an additional 260 million children into education systems. Recruitment of good quality teachers on that scale will take many years. Even in systems with teachers there are huge problems with poor quality, attendance, motivation and management. One study, based on random visits to Indian schools, found that 25 per cent of teachers were absent at any one time. In only half the schools was teaching in progress. About 90 per cent of the Indian education budget goes on teacher salaries: a very large portion of that is wasted.

Good teachers are the main constraint, the most precious scarce resources in the traditional education system. Of course it makes sense to train more teachers and make sure they turn up to teach. Yet radical frugal innovators like Ralph Bistany are not satisfied with how long this will take, nor with the variations in quality that will persist. Instead he foresees a world in which responsible children, supervised by adults, help one another to learn with the aid of technology when teachers cannot be found:

> Just imagine if we managed to create a school using technology where the cost per student is extremely small and yet the educational outcomes are high – the kids are totally bilingual, they are well read, excellent at math and science. We are trying to create a teacher-independent classroom. Because if you want to apply this at scale it is very difficult to do based on exceptional teachers. You cannot change the level of education worldwide if what you are doing is centred only on the ability of exceptional professionals.[45]

Ralphy Bistany is not alone is pursuing his dream of an education system that could deliver high quality at vast scale without relying on highly variable teachers leading traditional classes. In India and Africa, the radical educationalist Sugata Mitra has been developing teacherless, self-organised learning environments based on his experience with his Hole in the Wall computer-based learning project in which children learned using computers without support from teachers. Massive, open, online courses, known as Moocs, are spreading through the higher education field, pioneered by companies such as Coursera and Udacity. They are allowing tens of thousands of students to learn at the same time from a single teacher. Children are more likely to do well in school if they are ready for it. In developing countries that cannot afford dedicated children's centres, the most effective alternative is to train mothers in groups to become the first educators of their children. In Turkey, almost 250,000 mothers like Aziz Sagir have been through the 25-week Mother and Child Education Programme (Mocep), in which facilitators encourage mothers, who are often illiterate themselves, to take their children through simple exercises with numbers, words, pictures and writing. Studies show that children who start school having gone through the Mocep programme are far more likely to complete secondary school. Training mothers to become first educators is a simple and exemplary frugal innovation. Some of the greatest educational challenges are in small, rural multi-grade schools where a single teacher has to teach perhaps 60 children ranging in age from 4 to 13. Traditional methods, sitting children in a class together listening to a teacher presenting at the front of the class, do not work: children quickly become bored because the lesson is either too difficult or too easy. These rural schools tend to produce the worst results in any system. In Colombia, the Escuela Nueva programme has cracked this problem with a simple method that organises children into small groups, each with a workbook they follow for the subject in question. The teacher no longer has to teach 60 children, but instead facilitates ten groups of six, in which the children help one another. They do a more effective job. Escuela Nueva started in 1975 in 150 tiny rural schools. By 2011 it was operating in almost 17,000 Colombian schools and had been taken up in 19 countries, from Guatemala to Brazil. In that time its methods have been used with 5 million children. Far fewer students drop out from Escuela Nueva schools. They retain children of all abilities. Yet even so, pupils in Escuela Nueva schools outscore their counterparts in standard rural schools and Colombia is one of the few countries in the world where rural schools often perform better than their urban counterparts. It is not difficult to imagine how these components could be put together to create not just a lean school but a lean education system, in which teachers play a critical role, but supported by peer teaching, parents and technology.

* * *

Lean thinking is the first tool in the frugal innovator's toolbox: minimise waste; get things right first time; focus precious and costly resources where they create most value; avoid expensive, inflexible capital-intensive solutions; do without rigid bureaucratic systems which are costly and inefficient; enable cooperative problem-solving. Lean thinking started as a frugal innovation from a then marginal producer, Toyota, facing an extreme crisis. It has since been taken up imaginatively in Indian hospitals, which are among the most radical innovators in the healthcare industry, and among low-cost private schools, from the sophistication of the Sabis group to the epidemic of local, lean, low-cost private schools that are spreading through the slums and *favelas* of the developing world. The most interesting future models will be like MedicallHome and M-Pesa: they will be lean and networked, coordinating many dispersed contributors to create systems that would previously have needed a centralised production system. Those lean, networked solutions will often involve knowledge, skills and technology from the developed world, not least embedded in mobile telephone networks, but they will flower in the extreme, demanding and urgent conditions of the developing world.

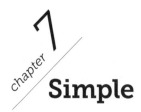

chapter 7

Simple

In Campeche, in the depths of the Mexican outback, surrounded by dense jungle, the residents of a small hamlet are achieving what would have seemed to be an impossible feat only a few weeks earlier. They are replacing the wooden shacks they used to live in with 12 proper homes, designed by architects, with toilets and bathrooms, lights and water, and all built in solid brick. The bricks are the miracle ingredient.

Even if they had been able to get to Mérida, the nearest city 200km away, these villagers would not have been able to afford to buy bricks from a building materials supplier. Their little village is dirt poor and also dirt rich: dirt is the only material they have in abundance. That was the starting point for Echale a tu Casa, a social business which has created a way for the poorest people to build their own homes using bricks they make themselves from the soil they find around them.

Making bricks from mud is an old idea. Generations of Mexicans have built homes using adobe. Echale a tu Casa has modernised that tradition with a machine that turns dirt into bricks simply by pressing a few buttons. The brick-maker is so simple most people can learn to operate it in 15 minutes. This is how it works.[46]

Dirt mixed with a small amount of sand and concrete is poured into the top of the machine, rather like beans into a giant espresso machine. The dirt is formed in four moulds. Then the operator presses some buttons to activate a gas-powered compression system which presses the dirt down to half the volume: 20 cubic centimetres of soil becomes 10 cubic centimetres of brick. After a few moments, four fully formed bricks pop out ready to be stacked. After drying for a couple of days, they are ready to be used.

One Echale machine, which costs about $20,000, can make enough bricks in a year to build 300 houses. Unlike other brick-makers it does not require electricity nor high temperatures, yet the bricks are 30 per cent stronger than cement, while making a house just as warm and quiet. The machine just needs a gas cylinder. The brick-maker is robust, mobile, adaptable, and so constantly in use, as it can be transported from village to village on the back of a pick-up truck. It is a flexible and adaptable machine in the best tradition of Toyota. A community working with three machines for a week can make enough bricks for 15 houses. It takes two more weeks to build a house. In little under half a year a community can be rebuilt, almost entirely through self-help. Those houses will include rainwater harvesting systems with a central purifier to create drinking water for 100 families. Instead of toilets there will be bio-digesters that produce fertiliser and methane for energy. By allowing families to build houses from home-made bricks they are less likely to cut down trees. Over the past 15 years communities using Echale machines have built 26,000 homes and extended a further 30,000.

The Echale a tu Casa machine, developed by founder Francesco Piazzesi, is a classic piece of frugal technology. As it does not rely on electricity it can be mobile and adapt to different settings. To be mobile it has to be relatively robust which means no complex, delicate moving parts. Above all it is simple. It does not have complex control systems that can go wrong. What makes the Echale brick-maker so simple is that it is part of a solution to a need, not just a standalone piece of technology. People do not want brick-makers; they want houses. Echale provides them with a simple solution to that need.

There is no point in having a lot of cheap bricks stacked up and not knowing what to do with them. A community has to have a plan for what it is going to build and in which order. That means they have to start collaborating with architects several months before they start making the bricks. Echale a tu Casa has found those design discussions are absolutely vital, otherwise people end up with inflexible brick houses that do not suit their needs and which cannot be remodelled as easily as a wooden shack. Some families want a larger living room because they need it to accommodate animals as well as people. Many want a very large porch because that is where they spend most of their time. Before they can start thinking about turning these plans into reality, the community has to save 30 per cent of the building costs and lodge that sum with a savings bank. That deposit then releases a government subsidy and a small mortgage which can be used to finance the construction. Working with Echale, the village can draw up a detailed plan to dig the foundations and prepare the other services. Often, when it comes to it, the houses are built through a community-wide effort. The houses are the product but in order to build them the entire community needs to come together. The social experience of coming together to save, plan and build is an important lasting legacy of the programme, alongside the houses. Most of the money spent on construction stays within the local community: they borrow money to pay themselves to build the houses. It takes perhaps ten years to pay off the mortgage. Echale a tu Casa takes a small margin – between 3 and 5 per cent of the $10,000 it costs to build a house – to invest in its own development, to buy more machines and maintain those it has. The next stage of the company's development will be to complete the cycle by setting up a micro credit arm which will organise the lending and borrowing at much lower rates than commercial banks. That will turn Echale a tu Casa into a complete circular economy: poor people will save, lend and borrow, from one another, to employ one another to build better homes, using Echale's machines. The system embodies all of the elements of frugal innovation. It is lean because there is no wastage: it uses locally available materials and the machines are constantly in use because they are mobile. It is social because it brings the community together: it's a friendly, convivial technology which encourages people to help one another. It's clean because it recycles existing materials, money and people: it gives poor people a way to build better homes in rural areas without cutting down more trees; it provides them with more environmentally sustainable homes, using mainly locally available materials and little energy. Simplicity is the fourth vital component which makes all of this possible. Echale a tu Casa's brick-maker is a simple product which is part of a simple system.

The Costs of Complexity

Complexity is invariably costly. Companies with many layers of management and so complex decision-making procedures invariably come with higher costs. Complex products that require special controls and components are more expensive to make, buy and maintain. To use them consumers often have to go through a lengthy and therefore costly process of learning. Complex products are confusing when there are no readily apparent underlying principles to fit all the parts together.[47] Products like video recorders become complex when those design principles are apparent to the designer but not to the end-user. Simple products, on the other hand, seem rather easy, obvious and inviting to use. They do not require special skills, learning, components, inputs, adaptors, nor supporting systems. The parts fit together easily and the product fits smoothly into daily life. Designing things to keep them elegantly simple is not easy.

Frugal innovation invariably involves simple products, for the reasons John Medea, a professor at MIT, sets out it in his design manifesto *Simplicity*: 'Simple objects are easier and less expensive to produce, and those savings can be translated directly to the consumer with desirable low prices. As evidenced by the extremely affordable line of simple products from the furniture retailer Ikea, simplicity benefits the frugal shopper.'[48]

The first step towards creating a simple solution is to create a simple product by reducing it to a basic core: the 20 per cent of features that create 80 per cent of the value. The low-cost airline easyJet has cut out most of the frills of flying to offer a bare-bones service which is cheap, safe and reliable – and that's it. Travelodge offers cheap hotel rooms which are little more than a clean bed, a cupboard and a shower. India is producing more of these simple, lean solutions than anywhere else. A prime example is the Tata Ace, a small truck designed to be 'cheap, nasty and rugged' which costs $5,000, half the price of other commercial vehicles. The Ace was developed with a minimal budget and a team of five designers, a fraction of what traditional car makers would spend. The small team and limited resources meant they could not design everything from scratch – they had to focus on what mattered most. As Ravi Kaushik, a director in GE's Indian healthcare business, put it: when customers are concerned about price, then designers have to work really hard to prioritise what is more important. 'Basically I use three buttons on my TV remote control, so when we develop a new device we work hard with users to identify the three most important features for them to use.'[49] To design this way you have to make tough choices but with the users in mind and often working with them to understand what will work.

In the late 20th century, innovation in the rich world became increasingly associated with adding features and functions to products to persuade existing consumers to upgrade to a new version of an existing product. To spend more they had to be offered more functionality at higher quality. As Clayton Christensen pointed out in *The Innovator's Dilemma*,[50] however, this move up market, to add more features to existing products, often clears the field for disruptive innovators to enter at the base of the market, offering more basic, lower-cost products, which appeal to new consumers who want products that are just good enough. Disruptive innovations are often more basic, low-cost versions of an existing product that expand the market. Low-cost airlines have been disruptive because it has made air travel affordable for the masses. Frugal innovators focus relentlessly on what counts most to the consumer; they strip out what is extraneous. The easiest way to simplify a product is to remove functionality. Another good way to discover simpler, less complex designs is to follow Paul Polak's advice to move forward by going backwards, recuperating and updating older, discarded ideas that come from a less technologically advanced time, when fewer options were available.

However, even a product with just a few features can still be dauntingly complex and confusing if it requires the user to read a large manual before they can start using it. The true test of a simple product is whether it affords itself to be used. A chair affords itself to be sat on: it invites the user to see that is what it is for. A lock on a door invites the bolt to be slid into place. A well-designed product offers subtle cues that make it easy to use. Creating this kind of affordance, however, is not just a matter of simplifying the interface and controls. It also comes from shrinking and concealing much of the complexity of a product, so reducing how much the user needs to know. The Apple iPod has only a few controls and the iPhone a single button. Almost all the complexity of these products is hidden from view. Complex products show off their multi-functionality; simple, frugal products hide their complexity.

Products are less costly to start using if consumers can learn how to do so from one another, mimicking each other's behaviour. No one needed a manual to start using Twitter or to send an SMS. The other way to make a product feel simple and obvious is to make it look and feel like something people already use. The master of this approach to product design is the Japanese designer Naoto Fukusawa, who has designed some of the best-selling products in Japan. One of Fukusawa's most famous products was an iconic, wall-mounted CD player for Muji, which was modelled on a kitchen extractor fan. So long as you have used an extractor fan with a pull cord, you know how to use the CD player. Fukusawa says he aims to design objects to be used 'without thought' by providing users with cues so they can work out how to use them almost automatically. Fukusawa's approach is to draw out the intelligence of users, with objects that feel familiar to people, that they already feel as if they know how to use. Complex and over engineered products often make people feel stupid.

That is one reason frugal innovators are inveterate and proud borrowers: when new products borrow from old they are easier to learn how to use. The super low-cost, handheld electrocardiogram developed in General Electric's lab in Bangalore, for example, incorporates a printer widely used on Indian buses. That has helped to reduce the cost per scan on the cheapest mobile versions of the machine to 25 cents. Therefore it is low-cost, simple to use and spare parts are easy to come by. Borrowing helps to make things simpler. Simple designs rarely deploy their own technical, professional language: more often they rely on the vernacular and colloquial, in architecture as in products. The Irish architect Dominic Stevens has created a wood-framed house that can be built for as little as €25,000 – depending on the price of the land – which is modelled on a traditional Irish cottage. The original low, long, Irish cottages were built by peasants with only local materials: rushes, wood, mud and stones. Stevens's wooden design draws on this frugal, vernacular tradition to create something that is simple, modern and traditional all at the same time. It is a home that can be built by a few people working together in a few weeks. That simple communal recipe for self-building might sound marginal in the developed world, yet the largest home-building movement in the world is among people building homes from scratch in slums and *favelas* where these recipes make perfect sense. As we will see, they also make sense in the developed world, in cities such as Freiburg in Germany and Almere in the Netherlands, each home to significant self-builder movements.

Simple products, however, can be confounded by complex and costly systems that let them down. As the designer Donald Norman puts it: 'Complexity can be tamed, but it requires considerable effort to do it well. Decreasing the number of buttons and displays is not the solution. The solution is to understand the total system, to design it in a way that allows all the pieces to fit nicely together.'[51] Systems that fit together make things simple; systems that do not make life a nightmare. Echale a tu Casa's brick-making machine would add to the complexity of life in villages if it just left them with thousands of bricks they did not know how to use. The simple machine is part of an overall system to plan, save and build homes. Systems trump products and simple systems trump even the best standalone product. Take e-book readers as an example. Sony took the brave step of launching the PRS-500 in September 2006, following hard on the heels of the failure of the Librie in Japan two years earlier. The PRS-500 was slim, well-designed, had a long battery life and its screen was easy on the eyes. It even came with its own bookstore, Connect.com, with 10,000 titles. The PRS-500 was hailed as the gadget that would change the entire publishing industry by changing how people read. It did not.[52] What did bring about that system change was a simple ugly duckling product: a dull functional machine with a strange name, the Kindle, from Amazon, an online retailer with no track record for designing electronic devices. The Kindle is the digital equivalent of the Tata Ace: it's cheap, ugly, portable and rugged. The Kindle was designed not as a product but as a solution: the point was to allow people to find, buy, download and start reading books as easily as possible. Readers could download books directly without having to go through a PC. Amazon was already a powerful force in book publishing. Cautious and conservative book publishers knew who they were dealing with. Moreover Amazon sacrificed some of its profit on e-book sales to get publishers to create digital books. Amazon made up this subsidy by selling the Kindle at a high margin. Readers flocked to the device because it was portable, convenient and gave access to a vast and growing library of books. It made buying and reading e-books simple. When the Kindle launched it came with a bookstore of 90,000 titles. Within a few years it was 330,000 and growing. Publishers gravitated to Amazon because they knew it would protect their rights and give them a share of the e-book profits. Amazon triumphed over Sony not because its e-book reader was a better product. On the contrary, the Kindle was only just good enough. The Kindle triumphed because it created a simpler system for both readers and publishers to meet their needs.

Simple products and systems will be essential in frugal solutions which do much more with much less. Simple products and systems, which are easy to make, cheap to buy and affordable to maintain, have an even greater appeal for consumers in emerging markets who want robust, portable, but well-designed products that are well adapted to often cramped homes and lives. Take a practical example: how to provide pre-school activities for children for $10 a year.

Education for $10 a Year

Madhav Chavan is frustrated and a little disoriented because he fears he is lost. His home city of Pune, in southern India, is growing so fast that new roads keep appearing almost without warning. It is 11.00 p.m. and we have just come from an education centre on the edge of the city where Chavan has been meeting with colleagues to thrash out new approaches to maths teaching for pre-school children. He has not eaten supper. When we arrive at his home, recently the beneficiary of another new road, he is engulfed by his cook and her family who press him to eat before they go off to bed. In the bare kitchen he chops a couple of shallots, which he eats raw with some dhal. We sit at a formica table, in hardbacked chairs. An hour later his wife calls from Mumbai to remind him that he has to get up early for a long drive and urging him to despatch me back to my hotel. He reassures her that he is taking good care of himself. An hour and a half later we are still talking. When I leave he is looking forward to four hours' sleep before doing it all over again.

That is the kind of drive that has helped turn Pratham, which Chavan helped to found and where he is chief executive, into the largest and most influential education NGO in India, and possibly the world. Chavan has not done this on his own. His partners include three formidable women: Farida Lambay, former vice-principal of the College of Social Work, the inspiration for many of Pratham's best ideas; Dr Rukmini Banerji, a graduate of Oxford and Chicago, who ran Pratham's programmes in several states before launching its highly regarded independent review of India's education system, and Usha Rane, who pioneered Pratham's early work with disadvantaged schools. This team has developed, out of necessity, experience and instinct, a frugal approach to education which has simplicity at its heart.

When they came together, Chavan had just emerged from running a government adult literacy programme in Mumbai which had failed largely thanks to the weight of bureaucracy. Lambay had managed to launch a few interesting but small-scale initiatives from the College of Social Work. They had a bit of funding from UNICEF and the support of the Municipal

Corporation of Mumbai. None of them had much experience in running pre-school programmes. Their first recruits were a handful of young, poorly educated women from the slums. Armed with that, they wanted to create universal access to primary education.

They had no money to create their own approach from scratch so they had no alternative but to borrow from what was already around. In the summer of 1993 a group of social workers had tried out a small summer programme called Didi – elder sister – in which older girls, who had just left secondary school, ran activities for children to keep them engaged with school and so ensure they did not drop out. For almost a decade the College of Social Work had been running a month-long programme called Vasantik Varga, designed to help children from the poorest backgrounds prepare for school: at most it reached perhaps 5 per cent of primary school children. At the time, it was the only pre-school programme run in the entire state of Maharashtra. It was through their efforts to expand this programme that Pratham became aware of the innovation that would make its name: the ultra low-cost *balwadi*.

Young local women who had completed their secondary education were trained in 12 half-day sessions to set up and run pre-school playgroups, using facilities provided by the local school. The women recruited the children and charged a nominal fee of Rs 5–10 to cover their costs. The women were eager to work: teaching in the local community is a vital route to a degree of independence and social mobility for women. Parents were keen to send their children to the *balwadis* and willing to pay. There were two constraints. These were the making of Pratham.

The first was space. There were not enough schools in the slums to run more than a handful of *balwadis*. As it was a municipal initiative the community development officers felt they had to use official, council spaces but these were not inviting for many mothers. Yet slums are built on the creative use of small spaces. Chavan and his team turned the problem on its head: 'In slums there are places of worship, social organisations, offices of political parties. We thought we could use those. If those were not available, the women could use their huts. And if they did not have a hut they could hold a group out in the open air.'[53] Pratham encouraged the formation of women's circles – Mahila Mandal – to support *balwadis* in their area.

The second constraint was skills. Chavan and Lambay knew that if they were to reach scale they had to keep their training simple and low-cost. If it became too lengthy and expensive they would not be able to run enough courses and their young women recruits would find it hard to keep up. So despite criticisms from educationalists that the training was too superficial, they stuck with the six-day programme, delivered as 12 half-days. They turned the best *balwadis* into training centres. The organisation generated its own capacity to grow as it expanded. Within a few years Pratham created its own training team, recruited from within its own ranks, which could train thousands of new women a year.

Chavan and Lambay reduced Pratham down to its basic ingredients: a young woman with basic training and a group of children, in a safe, local space, funded by parental contributions. Pratham spread by word of mouth, like a kind of epidemic. Women began to recruit their friends to run *balwadis*. Parents told one another about the new opportunities appearing in their localities. For several years Pratham was almost a virtual organisation, operating without its own office, so intent was its focus on bottom-up change. The simplicity of the basic model also allowed them to find a new route to scale.

'The challenge of generating a societal mission cannot be met unless one is willing to trust in the creativity and initiative of hundreds of thousands of people,' Chavan recalled. 'That meant we had to design something centrally which would allow people locally to take the initiative.'[54] Chavan calls this the Chinese restaurant model of scale and it is one widely used by frugal innovators. McDonald's has scaled by creating a template that its franchises must follow: everything is carefully scripted. Chavan knew this approach would be too prescriptive and inflexible; it would eliminate the scope for local know-how and improvisation that would be needed for the *balwadi* entrepreneurs to succeed and to connect with the localities. Chinese restaurants are as ubiquitous as McDonald's, yet there is no central template for them to follow. They follow similar, simple design principles but apply them in different ways, in different spaces and settings. The model is flexible enough to adapt to local circumstances and yet coherent enough to be easy to identify: no one walks into a Chinese restaurant unsure of what kind of food to expect. Pratham works in much the same way.

Chavan and his team have succeeded because they were resolutely determined to keep Pratham simple, to pare it down to its essential ingredients. There are no special facilities, lengthy training programmes, burdensome bureaucracy or heavy regulations. The *balwadi* is dirt cheap, very simple and easy to create: a young woman, with a school education, a passion to help children and a few days' training can get one up and running in a safe space within a few weeks.

Pratham's *balwadis* are not perfect but most are much better than anything else on offer to parents and children in many slums. By 1996 there were more than 400 *balwadis* in Mumbai. With the creation of the 45-strong training unit, numbers expanded fast: by the year 2000 there were almost 3,000. Now Pratham operates in cities across the country and reaches more than 3 million children a year through the *balwadis*: the Balsakhi programme supports poorer children at school to prevent them dropping out; the independent ASER review (impact in Hindi) mobilises 30,000 volunteers to conduct a household survey of educational outcomes in thousands of villages across the country. Now its flagship programme is Read India, a literacy campaign, which has retrained more than 600,000 teachers and government officials and mobilised 450,000 volunteers, to reach 33 million children across 19 states, covering 305,000 Indian villages. Academic studies show that Pratham's simple, local, low-cost, social support for children is far more cost-effective than lowering class sizes or introducing computers to schools. Dollar for dollar, Pratham is difficult to beat.[55]

All of this came from a group of people who, when they came together in 1994, had no experience of working in pre-school education and nowhere near enough money. As they were outsiders they were able to challenge conventional wisdom and to turn their main constraints – their lack of space and trained staff – into strengths. By doing without special facilities and trained teachers Pratham devised a model that can scale virtually everywhere in India. It is an ordinary innovation: nothing special was required.

One way to understand how Pratham has scaled is to think of it like a plant known as a radicant. Pratham is not like a tree, which has a central root system feeding a large main trunk off which branches grow. It is more like a strawberry plant, a radicant, which puts down its roots as it grows. Each time a radicant spreads a little further it puts down a little, local root, which sustains the local subsystem of the plant. That way the plant never spreads to areas that cannot sustain it and it continues to grow even if the first set of roots runs short of moisture. A radicant does not need a heavy-duty central core – a trunk – to keep it strong. Its strength lies in having lots of strong, local roots. That is the Pratham model: lots of little local roots. Pratham has created a national system of educational support for the poorest children in India by creating a model so simple it could spread easily and put down local roots. Most frugal innovators are radicants.

Saving Lives at Birth

A wave of simple, frugal technologies is about to sweep through health-care systems, starting in the developing world. Innovation in health technologies is inversely related to need. The health systems of high-income countries – the US, Europe and Japan – are awash with complex technologies. Almost 30 million MRI scans take place in the US each year. In the UK hundreds of thousands of people undergo radiotherapy for cancer each year. These technologies often help in the treatment of acute and life-threatening conditions: the CT scan, for example, is playing a vital role in improving care for stroke victims. Yet increasingly complex and specialised innovations in health technologies are also adding enormously to the costs of already overstrained healthcare systems. Patients expect, doctors offer and pharmaceutical companies provide new treatment innovations, almost without regard to the costs, and sometimes without a proper assessment of the benefits. As healthcare has become more specialised, this growing army of specialists has encouraged the proliferation of complex medical technologies. Most of those technologies are designed, made and used in the US, Europe and Japan, in health systems with ample funding, reliable energy supplies (the US health system accounts for 8 per cent of US greenhouse gas emissions) and a large workforce of well-trained professionals working in clean and controlled conditions in clinics and hospitals.

None of those conditions apply in the world where most people live and so not surprisingly there is a huge imbalance in access to health technologies: Japan has 90 times the MRI scanners of India, which has a population ten times as big. When attempts are made to close that gap by exporting rich world technologies, they invariably end in failure: one survey found that 40 per cent of equipment in hospitals in the developing world were out of service because they lacked back-up support, spare parts, reliable electricity and trained staff to use them.[56]

The health technologies that will address the needs of most people in the world will be designed for, with and increasingly in the developing world, in the situations where they will be used. They will be so simple they can be used without doctors, outside clinics.

A new wave of simple, easy-to-use healthcare technologies could transform life for millions of the poorest people in the world, much as better hygiene and antibiotics did in the developed world in the 20th century. The enormous constraints people face in the poorest parts of the world – lack of money and resources, electricity and water, people and skills, hospitals and clinics – are sharpening the pressure on innovators to find frugal health solutions which people can use in places where there are few nurses and doctors. To do so these solutions must be: cheap to make and to purchase but also to use and to maintain, in part because they do not need a ready supply of electricity and clean water; portable so they can be taken from a clinic to someone's home, or shared among villages, so they can be fully utilised; robust enough to withstand being knocked about, rained on, moved, possibly on a rickshaw, a bike or the back of a pick-up truck. Complex, expensive, fixed, heavy and fragile technologies, the kinds that might work in the perfectly controlled conditions of a clinic in Los Angeles or Munich, will not work in much of the world where they are most needed. They need simple, robust, reliable solutions.

One of the most important areas where this kind of innovation is needed to save millions of lives, is in childbirth. Each year there are 1.2 million late foetal, 150,000 maternal and 1.4 million early neonatal deaths. An additional 1.4 million women suffer acute complications in childbirth which threaten their lives. Millions of children are born prematurely, underweight and vulnerable to life-threatening complications. Many of these deaths are entirely preventable if only known solutions could be made available to mothers living in the poorest places.

Each year a third of mothers who die in childbirth do so because they haemorrhage and so bleed to death. In the developed world, such deaths are rare: only 6 in 100,000 mothers in Australia die as a result of haemorrhage in labour. That is because mothers can be given an injection of oxytocin into the uterus, which induces such powerful contractions that the bleeding stops. The active ingredients in oxytocin are not expensive: they cost about 50 cents per treatment. Yet, despite that, in the developing world haemorrhaging remains one of the main causes of death for mothers in childbirth. In Tanzania, for example, 790 maternal deaths per 100,000 births are due to haemorrhaging. The reason treatment with oxytocin is beyond the reach of these mothers is the way it has to be delivered – through an injection administered by a trained doctor or nurse. In most of South Asia and sub-Saharan Africa, nurses and doctors are in short supply: only half of births have a healthcare professional in attendance. That is not the end of the complications. To be safely injected the oxytocin needs to be stored in a refrigerator (expensive) and the refrigerator will need a reliable electricity supply (often not available). The treatment is simple and cheap enough, but the method of delivery is prohibitively expensive.

The solution would be to create a form of oxytocin that could be kept stable even in intense heat and which was easy to use for a mother giving birth at home with perhaps the help of a friend or neighbour. A team from Monash University in Australia has come up with just such a solution: an oxytocin aerosol spray which does not degrade outside a fridge and which can be administered at the press of a button, even by a mother who has just given birth entirely on her own. A woman in a remote village or a poor slum might be lucky to see a nurse once during her pregnancy, invariably early on. At that meeting the woman could be given an oxytocin spray to keep with her until it is needed. The Monash oxytocin aerosol is as simple to use as a deodorant and yet is not more expensive, dose for dose, than the traditional delivery system which requires nurses, fridges, syringes and electricity. In late 2012 Monash was awarded $1 million in funding from a group of funders orchestrated by the Gates Foundation to take their solution into human trials. If successful, the oxytocin spray – simple, cheap, robust and portable – could save the lives of millions of mothers. It came about by thinking of medical treatment through the lens of deodorants.

The smartest solutions are often the simplest and they often draw on ideas from other familiar products which can make a health technology instantly useable, without much thought, let alone training. Mother-to-child transmission of HIV is a huge issue in much of Africa. The best treatment is to give a baby anti-retroviral drugs within 24 hours of birth. Yet in traditional approaches this requires the drugs to be kept in a refrigerator and administered through an injection by a nurse. To overcome these constraints researchers at Duke University have developed a polyethylene pouch – a bit like a ketchup sachet from a fast food outlet – which can store anti-retroviral drugs outside a refrigerator for up to a year. The sachets can be easily distributed to pregnant women long before they give birth and then opened, with a sharp pull, when needed. If you have ever used a sachet of ketchup you will know how to administer this anti-retroviral.

Another example of frugal rethinking is an African effort to remake the humble ambulance, the workhorse of most healthcare systems. In the rich world ambulances are increasingly becoming more like mobile treatment centres, almost an emergency room on wheels, rather than a mode of transport. Ambulances like this only work, however, when there are decent roads, which means they are not much use for most people in the world where roads are usually potholed, rutted and bumpy, if they exist at all. The big opportunity – and need – is to go downmarket, to seek simpler, cheaper, more basic and robust solutions to the many millions of people who each year die for want of much more basic help. Devising those kinds of solutions only comes from working with the constraints of extreme conditions and lack of resources, looking sideways for new ideas and even backwards, as Paul Polak recommends, to find simpler, long-discarded solutions.

An ambulance does not need to be a large, well-cushioned, four-wheel vehicle. In the trenches of the First World War, clogged with mud, the most effective ambulances were motorcycles with a stretcher strapped to a sidecar. Motorcycle ambulances were nimble enough to get to places where traditional ambulances would get stuck. Innovators in Malawi adapted this old idea to create the e-Ranger, a motorcycle ambulance, with a sidecar compartment where a patient can either sit or lie down on a specially adapted stretcher. The e-Ranger is low-cost because it uses robust and affordable motorcycles commonly used across Africa. A four-wheel-drive ambulance, based on a Toyota Landcruiser, costs 19 times more than a motorcycle ambulance. Spare parts and maintenance are easy to come by. Running costs are much lower: fuel consumption is six times lower than that of a Landcruiser. Yet in three healthcare clinics where the e-Ranger was tested it reduced delays in getting pregnant women to a clinic by between 2 and 4.5 hours and led to a 30 per cent fall in maternal deaths. The e-Ranger is now being used in Kenya, too. The frugal ambulance of the future will be the motorcycle.

The simplest innovations are easy to use because they look and feel like something people already use. They are not designed for the special conditions of a healthcare clinic, but for everyday life: the motorcycle that becomes an ambulance; the aerosol that administers oxytocin; the ketchup sachet that holds anti-retroviral drugs. Some of the biggest opportunities will come from the adaptation and transformation of the mobile phone into a ubiquitous piece of health technology.

Frugal innovators devise simple, compelling services and solutions, which do not need long explanations: a way for young women to create a pre-school playgroup in their own home; a machine that makes bricks from dirt so people can build their own homes; a treatment for mothers bleeding after childbirth which works like a deodorant; an ambulance which is a motorcycle; a monitor for anaemia which works through a mobile phone.

They devise projects based on simple, compelling ideas that serve a clear need. Their solutions do not involve rocket science, even when they involve new technology. Complex solutions are costly, difficult to maintain, confusing and time consuming. Often they bewilder and disable people. Simple solutions tend to be easy to use, accessible, low-cost and inviting. They enable people to do more by enlisting their intelligence in creating the solution. Simpler is invariably better. That is the second key ingredient of the frugal innovator's toolkit.

8
Clean

Even as people in the developed world worry about the impacts of climate change, many more in the developing world worry about getting access to the most basic ingredients for a decent life: electricity and water. About 1.3 billion people, mainly in sub-Saharan Africa, India, Bangladesh and Pakistan, live without reliable electricity. The cost of their disconnection from basic utilities is huge. Life shuts down when the sun goes down; businesses close; reading stops; homework lies unfinished; doctors cannot see patients; people walk home along unlit roads. Electricity has become even more important in people's lives with the spread of the digital economy. There is little point in having a WiFi connection if there is no electricity to power a computer. Almost the first priority for modern people, rich and poor alike, is to find a place to recharge their mobile phone and so maintain their connection to the wider world. Every aspect of life – cooking, work, socialising, learning, trading – becomes constrained without electricity to light the way. More than a century after electricity supply systems became commonplace in the large industrial cities of the US and Europe, there is little prospect that those systems will reach the poorest households in the world using current technologies. These industrial era systems are too costly and cumbersome: they rely on large power plants that serve large numbers of relatively affluent consumers or they depend on hefty government subsidies. One estimate is that it would cost $665 billion to take electrification to the more than 1.3 billion who lack reliable electricity.[57] Not only that but these older systems depend on non-renewable sources of energy – coal, oil, gas – which also contribute to climate change.

So the innovation challenge in the very poorest parts of the world is to connect hundreds of millions more people to electricity at very low cost without adding to the toll of environmental destruction which traditional industrial systems have left in their wake. As we will see, that is also the challenge facing the cities of the developed world. In both places the solutions to this challenge will be frugal. One of the most instructive is in India where more than 480 million people in 125,000 villages lack reliable access to electricity.

Husk Power Systems (HPS) creates mini-utilities which serve a set of villages using a mini power plant fuelled by discarded husks left over from rice production.[58] An HPS system is capable of delivering power to hundreds of homes, for between six and ten hours a day: enough to power lights, fans, fridges, televisions and to recharge countless mobile phones. HPS embodies many of the principles of frugal innovation, in particular the way frugal innovators reinvent, recycle and reuse ideas, resources, technologies and even people. Frugal innovators are not proud. They do not have to invent an idea to use it. They excel at borrowing what works from other people. HPS emerged through a combination of ideas from the developed and developing world, formal and informal know-how, old and new thinking.

Husk Power Systems is the brainchild of an Indian power engineer, Gyanesh Pandey, who wanted to bring to bear the skills he had learned in the US electricity industry to provide electricity to the poorest villages in India. Pandey says he found the solution after a meditation course in rural India in 2006: rather than try to invent something from scratch, using new technologies such as solar power, he decided to reinvent an old, discarded technology – the biomass gasifier.

Gasification converts organic materials at high temperatures, without combustion and with a controlled amount of oxygen and steam, to create a synthetic gas. This syngas is a more efficient way to generate energy than direct combustion of the original fuel source – such as wood pellets – because combustion can be at higher temperatures. This also burns out corrosive ash elements such as chloride and potassium, allowing clean gas production from problematic fuel sources. Advocates of gasification argue it is carbon neutral because the production of the biomass in the first place removes as much CO_2 from the atmosphere as its eventual combustion produces.

Gasification pre-dates electrification: it is the technology that electrification displaced. In the developed world, coal and peat were used to create gas known as 'town gas' which was fed to street lights and homes. Yet if ever there was proof that ideas should never be completely discarded, it is gasification, which has come back from the dead several times, notably during periods such as the Second World War when petrol was expensive and in short supply. By 1945 an estimated 9 million trucks, buses and agricultural machines were powered by gasification all over the world. As conditions change so technologies that seem dated come back into fashion and so it might be with biomass gasification.

As conditions change so technologies that seem dated come back into fashion

The biomass gasifier provided an ideal solution in rural east India, because there was a ready supply of discarded fuel: rice husks were treated as waste. Husk Power Systems uses recycled material to power a recycled technology: that is why it can be installed at a cost half that of other renewable power systems, such as solar. It is also a highly social solution: about 400 households have to sign up to use the system before it can be installed, a form of collaborative consumption, akin to the way that projects are funded through Kickstarter, the leading crowdfunding platform. Households can opt for different service packages, like a mobile phone contract, ranging from powering several lights and appliances in a single home, to the lowest-cost and most popular package which allows two households to share a single bulb to light the courtyard between them. The cost per household is between $2 and $4 a month, affordable for all but the very poorest. By simplifying the technology, HPS has made the gasifier very low-cost to install and to run because local people can be trained to operate the plant. HPS helps local entrepreneurs to set up a plant as a mini-local utility, making a modest profit, and it has its own university to train a new generation of rural power engineers and entrepreneurs.

HPS is a model of frugal innovation: it is low-cost because it is lean, simple, clean and social all at the same time. By simplifying a known technology, the plant is easy enough to run for someone from an average Indian village: it does not need expensively trained professional engineers. (Another Indian mini-utility Decentralised Energy Systems India (DESI) claims that its biomass gasification system is even simpler and cheaper than HPS's.) It is more cost-effective than many home-based solar systems because it is social: it brings groups of villages together. The system is clean because it uses the waste from one system – agricultural rice production – as its fuel source. If frugal innovation were a political movement 'waste is fuel' would be one of its slogans. Like Pratham, HPS is a radicant organisation: it is putting down roots where it grows, with entrepreneurs serving their local communities. Pandey's plan was to have 1,770 plants installed by the end of 2013 in more than 7,000 villages serving more than 2 million households and 8 million-plus people, while offsetting more than 2.2 million units of CO_2. Each plant earns an average profit of about $335 a month or $0.07cents per kilowatt hour sold, enough to be able to pay off the loan the entrepreneur takes out through HPS to set it up.

A study for the International Finance Corporation (IFC) estimates that mini-utilities such as HPS could serve a market of $4 billion a year, filling in the large gaps left by traditional grids. In Cambodia, for example, community-owned mini-utilities serve 42 per cent of electrified households outside the capital, Phomn Penh. One of the largest mini-utilities in the world, Creluz in Brazil, uses run-of-river hydro-electric power to serve millions of people in 36 municipalities. Many of the greenest cities in the developed world – Copenhagen in Denmark, Malmö in Sweden and Freiburg in Germany – use local combined heat and power plants run as mini-utilities to provide energy for localities.

The market for home-based energy innovations, which are simultaneously cleaner and cheaper, is even larger: the IFC estimates that it could be worth $31 billion, the sum the poor of the world spend on kerosene, candles and disposable batteries. Simple, clean and cheap innovations abound in this space. The most basic is a simple coal stove, made by the Ghanaian company Toyola, which generates clean heat for cooking. More than 2 million people a year die of diseases linked to open and coal fires in their homes. Morocco has achieved close to universal electrification by extending its existing electricity grid and supplementing it with home-based solar systems which cost anything between $100 and $500. Grameen Shakti in Bangladesh is one of the most successful home solar system providers in the world with a turnover of more than $80m and more than 1 million systems installed for clients. The organisation provides after-sales service and back up through a network of 1,068 village branches which employ almost 10,000 people. Grameen Shakti is also radicant: through a simple, easily replicable model it puts down roots as it grows, using local people to fund, run and maintain the systems it installs.[59] Solar lanterns made by companies such as Nest, Greenlight Planet and Barefoot Power are spreading fast, to provide light to poor homes but also to recharge the ubiquitous mobile phone. Nuru lights created in Rwanda are recharged by entrepreneurs riding a stationary bike of the kind used in gyms around the world.

These frugal innovators, like Gyanesh Pandey of HPS, have pulled off a trick we will need to play over and over again in the future: they meet the needs of many millions of people, at low cost, while also being environmentally restorative. They do this not by being heroic and egotistical. They do not seek to create from scratch a product which might bring them fame and fortune. Instead their frugal approach to innovation relies on 're'-thinking: *re*use, *re*cycle, *re*purpose, *re*new.

Frugal by Nature

Creating a more inclusive capitalism means finding ways to include more people in its benefits as consumers and workers. However, if that goal were to be achieved using our existing, heavy-duty industrial systems it would bring with it environmental destruction on an even greater scale. So the challenge is to rethink the systems we use to provide the most basic goods and services, such as water, electricity and energy, so they can reach more people but with much lower environmental impact. Genuinely frugal innovation has to be clean as well as lean, simple and low-cost, otherwise low-cost solutions simply breed more demand and so exact a greater environmental toll. The consequence of this is that frugal innovation, to be really successful, also has to be systemic: it has to be about redesigning entire systems, end-to-end, not just individual, standalone products and services, such as low-cost heart operations or super-cheap ECG machines. The best place to look for the principles that should guide these new systems is systems that are clean and frugal by nature.

Natural systems use and synthesise materials in ways that are compatible with other living systems: they do not take resources from nature and then dump waste back into it. Instead natural systems have a circular, closed logic to them: they use energy and materials sparingly and turn waste from one process into fuel for another.[60] Despite what we would regard as impossible limits, natural systems manage to make complex things at very low temperatures, without using harsh chemicals or artificial high pressure. Compared with nature even our most sophisticated industrial systems are clumsy and crude. The inner shell of the abalone, for example, is two times tougher than ceramic fired in a high-temperature kiln and yet the abalone uses no heat to make the shell that hard. Termites create complex towers that stay at a constant temperature, about 86 degrees Fahrenheit, using the natural air conditioning of ventilation. Spider silk, ounce for ounce, is five times stronger than steel. Mussels can stick themselves to a rock, without a primer, using a remarkable adhesive tether – byssus – which works under water. All these products, moreover, fade back to where they came from after use, whereas our astounding feats of chemistry are often overengineered: plastics live on for hundreds of years after they were last used. If we were able to follow the design principles of the mussel and the abalone, then we could create not just inclusive and low-cost systems, but ones that were clean and even restorative, helping replenish natural systems rather than depleting them.

The industrial systems of the future should take their design cues from these natural, restorative and circular systems. Productive systems have to import energy from somewhere, but the best sources are local, current and renewable. Rather than relying, as industrial systems do, on ancient energy that is stored in fossil fuels, natural systems gather and use current sources much more efficiently. The purchasing agent for the sun's energy is a vast natural solar array of leaves, plants and algae which turn the sun's light into chemical bonds with amazing efficiency. Where industrial, consumer systems are profligate with energy and waste, losing vast quantities of heat in storage, transmission and use, natural systems excel at conserving energy as much as possible, using it sparingly and to good effect.

Natural systems limit the amount of waste they generate through lean and just-in-time systems which have evolved successfully because they only use what they need and no more. Evolution has rewarded frugality. Successful natural ecosystems use materials sparingly; shopping locally (to use as little energy as possible), they use resources within easy reach; they tend to favour solutions that weigh as little as possible and are appropriate for their context. Natural systems tend not to overengineer complex systems that involve costly maintenance and last long beyond their useful life.

Nor do natural systems tend to foul their own nests in the way industrial systems do by generating vast quantities of waste and pollution. The lesson of natural systems is that if you do produce waste, do so in a way that others close by can use as a source of fuel or as an input into another process. The corollary is that different parts of a single ecosystem have to be closely related and integrated, rather than specialised and fragmented. Waste that flows from one system should ideally go straight into another. Products should be designed so they can easily be taken apart and reused, refurbished, recycled or reincarnated in another form. Clean systems have to be integrated and circular, designed to capture waste and recycle it. To do so they must be interdependent. [61]

Natural systems are frugal because when they are mature, like a redwood forest, they do not dash for growth. Getting big at all costs is not the key to success in the long run. Finding the right proportion so that you fit into the niche that sustains you is much more important. Mature ecosystems endure because they are evolved for the long term, for endurance and resilience rather than rapid throughput. They are steady and stable, reusing their resources rather than trying to expand to capture new territory. They achieve this through diversity and interdependence, to make sure there are enough different kinds of plants and animals to occupy every possible productive niche, to make the most of what is there. They are rich because they are internally diverse rather than expansive and resource-intensive.

Industrial systems take, make and waste resources, in at one end and out the other. Frugal, clean systems are circular, closed loops in which nothing is wasted. Their watchwords are not create, make, mine and waste, but reuse, recycle, refurbish, restore. A restorative economic system, which limits environmental damage in the first place and repairs it quickly when it happens, would direct innovation to conserve resources rather than to deplete them.

The industrial revolution gave us gears, hydraulics, engines and fuel to vault over and past natural systems, powered by animals, wind and water. The more we have come to rely on these technical, industrial systems, the more they have rewarded the way of thinking that makes sense of them: rational, transactional and quantified. In the 19th and still for much of the 20th century, natural limits to these systems must have seemed a long way off. Resources were plentiful. Virgin materials could be found through expansion, going wider and deeper. The earth's capacity to absorb the waste these systems generated could almost be taken for granted. Nature had provided a seemingly free, limitless disposal facility. Those limits to the way we acquire, use and waste energy and other resources are now becoming pressing, economically, socially and environmentally. We can no longer afford to live with profligate and predatory systems that take little or no account of the natural systems upon which they depend.

To meet expanding needs but within tightening resources constraints we will need innovation guided by an ethic of 're': reuse, recycle, restore. That means reusing existing ideas and technologies because they are cheap to develop and proven in practice; piggybacking on existing infrastructures rather than building all-new ones; connecting up systems so the wasted heat from one can become the energy to fuel another; designing products so they can be broken down to be reused, over and over again. 'Re'-thinking will be as vital to tackling big social challenges as pure creativity, inventing new things from thin air. Let us look at three crucial examples of where 're'-thinking is needed and opportunities for innovation abound: the relationships between water, food and cities.

Every Drop Counts

Control over water has been central to the success of societies for centuries and ours is no different. From irrigation for agriculture, to power for industry, trade on rivers and clean water for urban consumers, the ability to control and provide water has been vital politically, economically and militarily. We might be able to find substitutes for coal and even oil, but not for water, which is why there is hardly a freshwater source, river or lake in the world, that is not being managed by man. Now those efforts, which rely on the heavy-duty industrial infrastructure of dams and bore holes, pumps and pipes, are reaching the limits of their effectiveness.[62]

The earth is mainly made of water and yet only a tiny fraction is fresh water and most of that is currently trapped in the ice caps. Much of the remainder lies deep underground in aquifers that are inaccessible. Groundwater, in rivers and lakes, the sources we mainly use, accounts for just a tiny fraction of 1 per cent of all the water on earth. Our sophisticated, complex urban civilisations depend on our ability to exploit the tiny sliver of the world's water that goes through the remarkable cleaning process of evaporation, desalination and precipitation. As the world's population grows, and particularly its cities, so competition to control this tiny margin of resources is becoming more intense.

Three-quarters of our water use goes to irrigation to grow food. Between 2,000 and 5,000 litres are needed to grow a bag of rice using current techniques. A pound of wheat takes 250 gallons of water. A hamburger needs 800 gallons. A 1-litre plastic bottle needs 4 litres of water in its production. When you buy a litre of bottled water you are really buying five litres.[63] Feeding the world's expanding population has been a huge achievement: food production has more than doubled in the past 20 years mainly thanks to the introduction of high-yielding varieties of crops. Yet world water usage has tripled. Our growing array of dishwashers, toilets, power showers, wet rooms, washing machines, jet sprays and lawn sprinklers has made its own contribution to this rise in water usage, but the main factor is food production. Access to water is now a more significant constraint on food production than land. Taking water from remote and underdeveloped regions and delivering it to populous and fast-growing cities requires vast, complex, costly and environmentally damaging feats of engineering. Drilling for water deep underground and pumping it to the surface uses lots of energy. Water is surpassing oil as the scarcest resource in the world. As a result water is also becoming a flashpoint for conflict both between but more often within states, not least because water inequality is growing. More than 1 billion people lack access to a gallon a day of safe drinking water. Half of the world's hospital beds are occupied by people suffering water-related illnesses. Diarrhoea kills more than 1 million children each year.[64] Tens of millions of children miss school just to get water for their families, and in Africa and Asia it is commonplace for women to walk 6 kilometres a day to get their family clean water. Even when they do get clean water, the poor often pay more per litre than the rich. More than 2.2 billion lack the water needed for decent urban sanitation. Yet in the US the average person uses the equivalent of 150 gallons a day.

For the first time in modern history society's thirst for fresh water, driven by population growth and agriculture, is set to outstrip supply using current technologies and forms of organisation. Until now man's impact on water-systems has been modest and localised, limited to the flow of rivers serving a city. Yet now across heavily populated parts of the world much of the groundwater on which society depends is heavily depleted by overuse and pollution. Water shortages could hold back growth and development, provoking growing inequalities and tensions. One of the biggest innovation challenges of the present century will be the reinvention of our relationship with our most basic, life-enhancing resource: water. Those places that find the most effective, innovative solutions to this looming crisis, will also come out as winners. They will be more economically productive, socially inclusive and politically stable.

The traditional response is to think big and heavy: larger dams, deeper wells, more powerful pumps, to take more water over longer distances. Politicians love dams: iconic, grand projects which symbolise their power. In the US dam-building was part of the Keynesian recipe that helped the economy out of the Depression in the 1930s. In the developing world dams signal progress, not least because of the hydro-electric power they generate. Yet even the World Bank, the main past sponsor of vast dam-building projects, now acknowledges that their economic, social and environmental costs often outweigh their benefits: more than two-thirds of dams built to irrigate agricultural land, for example, deliver less water than projected. Dam-building is prone to large cost overruns. Instead of seeking to take this old technological regime even further, the solutions of the future will lie in smaller, distributed, intelligent and connected systems which: allow rainwater to be harvested and used where it falls; develop low-cost, low-energy ways to turn salt water into fresh water; encourage frugal forms of consumption by industry and households; ensure as much water as possible is recycled for further use, thus reserving as much fresh water as possible for human consumption. Frugal innovation will be absolutely central to creating the next generation of water systems. Once again the place to look for the early exemplars of these future systems is in the margins, not the mainstream.

Clean, Green and Blue

One source of inspiration is low-cost products designed to provide low-income consumers with drinkable water, even when the supply around them is polluted. Tony Flynn, a lecturer in ceramics and materials at the Australian National University, has designed an ingenious and simple clay filter mixed with coffee grounds, which can be made from materials available in most localities and filters out most pathogens. When the clay is fired, for example in a kiln using clay and dung, the coffee grounds burn away creating small holes which allow water through, but not pathogens.[65] The Life Straw, designed by Swiss company Vestergaard Fransden, costs just $20 and filters about 18,000 litres in its lifetime, with no power other than the suction from human lungs.[66]

One of the best-known examples is the Tata Swach, which was billed as one of the cheapest household water filters in the world when it was launched in 2009. Tata's machine – Swach means clean in Hindi – uses a mixture of traditional and high-tech nano materials to purify 3–4 litres of drinking water per hour at a cost of about $0.002 per litre. Each filter costs about $7 and can purify about 3,000 litres. Tata is hoping the Swach will reach more than 200 million households, often in rural areas, bringing them the realistic prospect of clean, affordable drinking water. More than 1,000 children in India die each day due to waterborne diseases.[67]

The supply side equivalent of these low-cost, end-of-the-pipe water filters, is the wide array of simple pumps which are designed especially to help small-scale farmers get access to water. There is the Rovai rope pump, the bamboo treadle pump designed by IDE and Kickstart's successful moneymaker pump aimed at subsistence farmers.

Laudable as these products are, they only offer at best a partial solution. End-of-pipe solutions such as the Tata Swach are built on the assumption that the cheapest solution – clean water at source – will not be available. Standalone pumps might help farmers to help themselves, but effective long-term solutions will turn on how shared solutions for better use of a common resource emerge. We need not only frugal products but frugal systems and those systems will often deploy a mixture of very old and very new technologies.

One such technology will be desalination to obtain fresh water from seawater, a technology first developed by the US Navy in the Second World War for troops trapped on desolate Pacific islands. For most of its life desalination has been prohibitively expensive because of the energy required to push seawater through membranes that catch the salt particles. Over the past two decades, however, membrane technology has improved markedly and so energy costs have fallen in step. The most efficient desalination plants in the world, in California and Israel, deliver clean water for less than $0.50 a litre. But if desalination could be combined with solar power, then the costs could fall even further. Potentially limitless amounts of fresh water could be created.

The father of that idea is probably Charlie Paton, a likeable British inventor, in the best traditions of the amateur back-room boffin who tries to change the world from a garden shed with a brilliant idea that gets exploited by someone else who gets rich in the process. When I first met Paton in the early 1990s, he was consumed by the idea of creating a greenhouse, more like a tent, which could conjure fresh water from thin air. Like most radical innovators, Paton was also often dismissed as slightly bonkers. Yet his idea was compelling, simple and elegant. Cold seawater would be evaporated from cardboard pads to cool and condense the moisture in the air to produce fresh water. Paton and his family were so committed to the idea they built, by hand, a prototype greenhouse in Port Augusta, South Australia, which had thousands of handmade plastic pipes dripping water onto cardboard powered by self-built solar panels. Paton's tent seemed to be the equivalent of perpetual motion: a solar-powered system for making water out of thin air. The tent was not just a product – like the Tata Swach – but an interlinked, circular system for generating fresh water for growing food.

Paton's vision, the Seawater Greenhouse, is avowedly low-tech and principled: the idea is that it does not need an external energy supply other than the sun. Yet it caught the attention of an ambitious former Goldman Sachs banker Philipp Saumweber who had just joined his family's Munich-based agricultural business. Soon after he became immersed in the business, Saumweber realised agriculture was mainly an energy and water industry, with food as its product. That made him interested in alternative sources of fresh water and energy, which in turn led him to Paton, working away in a converted three-storey bakery on the edge of London Fields, now possibly the trendiest patch of park in London. Saumweber decided Paton's technology was too promising to ignore, despite its several failures. It had an elegant way to make fresh water and to cool the greenhouses at the same time while using very little energy.[68]

Paton and Saumweber formed a joint venture but it did not take long for them to fall out. Paton wanted to stick to the principles of solar-powered sustainability, even if that meant people eating slightly oddly shaped tomatoes because loss of power at night affected how they grew in the cold. Saumweber wanted to build a sustainable business which meant delivering what supermarkets demanded. That entailed installing a gas boiler to provide heat for the greenhouses during cold nights, to make sure the produce grew without becoming blemished and misshapen in such a way that supermarkets would reject. It also meant bringing in technologies from Germany and Switzerland and a young ambitious team, the very antithesis of Paton's slightly down-at-heel, Heath Robinson-like ethical innovation.

The Sundrop farm Saumweber created miles out in the South Australian desert might be the equivalent for 21st century production systems of Henry Ford's first factory in Dearborn. The principles it employs should inform many others following in its wake. A 75m line of motorised parabolic mirrors follow the sun all day to focus heat on a pipe that contains a sealed-in supply of oil. The heated oil warms a tank of water drawn from the sea which is only 100m away. The oil brings the seawater up to 160 degrees centigrade and steam from this drives turbines which in turn provide electricity. Some of the electricity heats the greenhouses during the night but most of it powers a desalination plant which creates 10,000 litres of fresh water a day. The air in the greenhouses is kept humid and cool by trickling water over a wall of honeycombed cardboard evaporation pads through which air is driven by wind- and solar-powered fans. The produce is effectively organic because it uses no pesticides and the crops are grown hydrologically. The greenhouses have flights of in-house bees to do their stuff, cross-pollinating the plants.

Paton continues to win plaudits and awards. He worries that his brilliant idea has been debased by ambitious young people who have put money before principles. Saumweber can realistically claim to have saved a brilliant, amateur idea from a lifetime of obscurity by applying the business skills needed to take it to scale. At the end of 2013 Sundrop was building an £8 million, 20-acre greenhouse 40 times bigger than the current one, which will produce 2.8 million kilograms of tomatoes and 1.2 million kilograms of peppers. More Sundrops are on the way in places with similar conditions, like the Gulf States of the Middle East. In conditions where there is ample sun and seawater this seems a potentially infinitely scalable solution to grow not just vegetables but protein too, in controlled conditions enjoying seemingly limitless supplies of fresh water at very low cost.

Charlie Paton's simple, elegant system for creating fresh water at low cost is one of a family of solutions that depend on intelligently recycling water in the atmosphere, that tiny margin of rainwater, condensation and fog, on which we depend. Industrial technologies rely on capturing that water once it has fallen to earth in rivers and lakes, but frugal solutions focus on capturing it in leaner, more direct ways, where and when it first falls.

In the high Atacama desert in Chile where there is fog from the Pacific but little rain, people have created fields of giant plastic sails to catch the water in the air. A fog farm of 75 sheets can produce enough water for a village to live on. In Gansu province in inland China most people have access to clean, fresh water, without being connected to a mains supply, thanks to ancient cisterns in the cellars of their houses where they hold harvested rainwater. In Tunisia olive trees are grown in their thousands fed by meskats, local reservoirs the size of a tennis court. In India, Iran and Afghanistan small local radicant solutions – ponds and tanks – are being revived. Rainwater harvesting is becoming akin to social movement, spreading among farmers and villages. According to the UN Environment Programme's International Environmental Technology Centre in Osaka, these local self-help solutions could be scaled up to help hundreds of millions of people, in rural and urban areas, get access to clean water.[69]

Rainwater harvesting is a classic frugal solution: it is lean (it captures the rain close to where it is needed rather than drawing water from a vast central inventory); simple (it uses technologies that the average small-scale farmer can maintain); social (often it involves people sharing a resource like a pond or tank), as well as being clean (it recycles locally available resources).

Pepsee

When these locally efficient forms of water collection are combined with the efficient use of water then there are the makings of a frugal system. One of the most important instances of this is the emergence of low-cost, drip-irrigation systems in farming. Irrigation to grow food makes the largest single call on our water resources, yet many of the traditional systems, based on irrigation canals and sluices, are very crude, delivering floods of water, in the wrong places, in large quantities, much of which then evaporates off. The most efficient irrigation systems drip small quantities of water in a very controlled way right to the plants' roots. The basic starter kit for a drip-irrigation system can cost between $500 and $2,000, well beyond the means of most farmers. Indian farmers had a traditional alternative, to drip-irrigate using bamboo pipes with small holes drilled into them. Some farmers use discarded bicycle inner tubes but these are too expensive for most people. The most cost-effective solution to date is a classic frugal innovation: the Pepsee.[70]

All over India street vendors sell flavoured frozen water – ices – in small thin plastic tubes, which people then suck on, known as a Pepsee. Each Pepsee is made from a long tube and when those tubes have small holes made in them they become perfect for drip-irrigation. It is not clear who first came up with the idea of turning the ubiquitous Pepsee into an irrigation system, but once they did the solution spread like wildfire. As it spread, so farmers developed the system to make it more effective: the clear plastic tubes tended to grow algae and go green in the sun, so instead Pepsee rolls for farmers are now black. Pepsee ices are sold in such large quantities that the plastic tubing was already very low-cost: a one kilogram roll costs just Rs 50. That means a farmer can create a drip-irrigation system for just $50 per hectare, a tenth of the lowest-cost alternative. The rolls are so light they can easily be moved so farmers do not have to buy new systems to water more land.

When frugal systems for collecting and recycling rainwater are combined with frugal systems for using it for irrigation, then there are the makings of a frugal system for the supply and demand of water. To make frugal systems work, however, a third component is needed: an organisation to knit the two together. In most places in the developed world that role is carried out by utilities owned or regulated by the government. In much of the developing world social entrepreneurs are pioneering local, frugal water solutions which are sustainable because they are designed to work for consumers with limited resources.

The Water Shop

A prime example is the spread of mini-water treatment plants and local water networks in areas that are too small, too poor and too informal to be of interest to large utilities. Often in these poor communities the water is so brackish and deeply polluted that traditional water filters, even the Tata Swach, are not powerful enough to provide clean water. In these places poor people pay a high price for clean water. Shared, local water purification plants are one cost-effective solution. In India two social enterprises – Naandi and Sarvajal – have taken their lead from the spread of the low-cost, pre-paid mobile phone to create local water kiosks which people draw water from using a pre-paid card. A mini-water purification plant of this kind can serve a village or a small area in a slum.[71]

Naandi was the first in the market with mini-water treatment plants that cost about $15,000 to install, with most of that investment coming from government grants, philanthropy and community donations. Sarvajal followed in Naandi's wake but managed to drive down the installation cost to $3,000 by reverse engineering a bare-bones, simplified version of the kit and housing it in an existing building rather than building one from scratch. A Sarvajal plant can produce between 500 and 1,000 litres of clean water per hour, at a cost of 2 to 6 cents per litre, affordable even for the poorest households. Sarvajal has financed its growth by becoming a low-cost business: a local entrepreneur can purchase a Sarvajal franchise for $950. After paying Sarvajal 40 per cent of the revenue, most entrepreneurs still make a good living.

Sarvajal has all the benefits of a frugal solution: it is lean (centralised purchasing of equipment allows economies of scale, while remote monitoring of the plants helps engineers to prevent costly breakdowns); simple (because its plants operate a bare-bones, slimmed-down purification plant based on existing buildings); social (the economics work so long as most of a village start using the kiosk) and it is clean (it makes water drinkable at affordable cost). Sarvajal's kiosks serve more than 1,000 villages with more on the way. When plants like this are combined with decentralised, small-scale water networks then it is possible to see how local solutions to water needs could spread to scale.

All of the ingredients are available for much more frugal, localised water systems, from supply to distribution and consumption: rainwater harvesting; water recycling; solar-powered desalination and seawater cooling systems for condensation; water purification systems using flora and fauna; mini-water plants and distribution systems to serve small, poor communities economically; consumer technologies, such as low-cost drip-irrigation systems, to make sure water is used with great care as a scarce commodity. All of that might seem far-fetched and implausible in the rich, urban and developed world that already has an infrastructure of reservoirs, tunnels and pipes. Yet nothing could be further from the truth: the most successful, sophisticated cities of the future will develop frugal water systems. Indeed some of the most successful already do and they are not in the developed world.[72]

Singapore: Crisis, Constraint and Innovation

In the early 1960s Singapore's survival was threatened by water shortages of the kind that now overshadow many cities in the world. Severe droughts forced widespread rationing of household supplies and limited industrial output. Singapore's basic water infrastructure had been installed in the late 19th and early 20th centuries by British engineers who dammed-up streams and built reservoirs and municipal waterworks. As Singapore's economy grew so the land taken up for clean water catchment for the reservoirs became more commercially valuable. Expanding the water supply using traditional technologies was impossible. Singapore was at an impasse.

The first leg of Singapore's strategy to ease its water crisis was to focus on rainwater. Singapore gets more than double the global average rainfall but most of it washes away. Rather than hope to serve urban areas using water from distant reservoirs, Singapore set out to turn the city itself into a water catchment system feeding rainwater into a network of localised reservoirs and tanks which are hidden beneath school playing fields and motorway flyovers. They are connected through a computer-controlled system of tunnels and pipes. To make sure the water flowing into these tanks is as clean as possible, the authorities led an attack on sources of industrial and household pollution which is one reason why dropping chewing gum there is still a crime. Singapore keeps its streets clean because that is where its water comes from. The city is its own reservoir. The cleaner the streets, the cleaner the water.[73]

The second ingredient was the NEWater strategy launched in 2002 which aimed to recycle as much industrial water as possible. Recycling water has a powerful multiplier built into it. When one drop of clean water is recycled it can create half a drop of clean water. When that drop is recycled it creates a quarter of a drop. If this process of recycling is continued a single drop of water can eventually produce another drop. In Singapore recycled water is mainly used in industry and for domestic use (such as for flushing toilets) but not for human consumption. That decreases demand on Singapore's very precious supplies of truly fresh water. The first large-scale recycling plant was set up in 2002 and ten years later this was supplying 30 per cent of Singapore's water demand. Recycling has halved the reservoir capacity Singapore needs.

The third part of the strategy was a big investment in one of the most sophisticated desalination plants in the world, known as Tuas. Singapore has very little water on land but it is surrounded by the sea. Desalination has been a part of Singapore's water strategy since the 1970s but the energy costs involved always weighed against it. Desalination can also leave behind a destructive, highly concentrated brine. In 2005 a new desalination plant was commissioned using the latest in reverse osmosis technologies that allow fresh water to be produced at low temperatures, with minimal energy and limited side-effects.

Singapore is still not self-sufficient in water: it relies on imports from Malaysia. However, it is far more independent than it was thanks to a strategy that involves urban rainwater harvesting on a massive scale, large-scale water recycling and one of the largest desalination plants in the world. Singapore shows that frugal innovation to make the most of scarce water supplies is not a strategy mainly for low-income communities: it should be at the heart of a modern, urban sustainable economy. Like all frugal innovators Singapore used the tight constraints it was working under to its advantage to trigger a search for solutions that turned conventional thinking on its head. Singapore's frugal approach to supplying water was matched by innovation and social change on the demand side. In the 30 years to 1994 Singapore's population doubled to close to 4 million, but its water demand rose by a factor of four. Since the mid-1990s, however, a social movement to conserve water for the national good has taken hold. This, combined with the introduction of water meters, tougher pricing and low-cost technologies to help households reduce their water usage, has reduced domestic per capita water consumption. Since 1994 Singapore's economy has grown by about 5 per cent per annum, its population growth has been 2.2 per cent a year, but water demand has risen by only 1 per cent.

Cities That Feed Themselves

We mainly use water to grow food, to supply consumers in the city. If we could combine frugal water systems with frugal, urban food systems, then we might have a complete, new cycle of water and food production. This would involve cities devising ways to feed themselves more, from close to the city. Once again we can learn from history.

In the 17th century the farmers around London then working in the open countryside did not have the skills for profitable large-scale vegetable production. Londoners had to import their vegetables from the Netherlands. Then Dutch Protestants fleeing persecution found safe haven in London and brought with them the secrets of how to produce cheap and plentiful vegetables: the key was manure laid out in hotbeds, covered with soils into which fruit and vegetables were planted.[74] The manure nourished the plants and released waves of heat so they grew more quickly. That new, improvised technique meant that a small plot of land – about 3 acres – could sustain a profitable vegetable business and so the trade of market gardening was born. By 1662 London was peppered with 10,000 market gardens. Battersea was famous for its asparagus; there was a Fulham parsnip and a Hackney turnip. In 1665 Dung Wharf was set up to provide these gardens with manure – human and animal – shipped along the Thames, the boats returning with fruit and vegetables for the markets in the centre of town. At the start of the 17th century London could not feed itself. By the end of the century it could and it did so by recycling its own waste to make small plots of land highly productive. Could a similar system – recycling waste and using local water supplies – feed a modern city now? Yes it could.

A modern version of the city fed by urban market gardens can be found in a marginal city, outside the mainstream, which faced a crisis threatening its future: Havana.

Cuba suffered a profound shock when the Berlin Wall fell and suddenly the market in the former Soviet Union for its overpriced sugar dried up. The US trade embargo meant that Cuba found itself largely isolated in the world economy and with large industrial farms, with combine harvesters and tractors, which no longer had export markets. The decline in Cuba's foreign earnings meant they could not import food as they once had. The crisis had a direct impact on how Cubans grew and ate food. In 1989 the average Cuban was eating 3,000 calories a day. By 1993 it was closer to 1,950.[75] Yet Cubans then responded to the belt-tightening by starting to grow food in new ways, on small private farms and in thousands of pocket-sized urban market gardens. They could not use imported fertilisers so these small farms were de facto organic. In Havana alone there are more than 200 *organopicos*, urban gardens, on formerly vacant lots, which employ local people to grow food, supported by a network of specialist agronomists. Across the country there are thousands of these local, cooperative urban gardens. Thanks to the extreme conditions of its isolation, Havana has created the world's largest model of a semi-sustainable, urban, organic agriculture which uses only limited amounts of energy, oil and chemicals. Singapore is a city that largely waters itself; Havana is a city that largely feeds itself. When these two models are combined, the clean, low-cost ways of growing food for cities – well vegetables – become a real possibility.

Is Low Cost Frugal?

Fully frugal innovation is not just ultra low-cost. It must be low cost *and* clean, meeting people's needs while using fewer resources per capita. That often means looking not just at the product but whether the system as a whole is frugal. A frugal product can be part of a profligate system. To see the significance of the distinction between frugal and low-cost products and systems, take the example of a classic frugal innovation, the container, and the system it gave rise to, containerisation.

On 1 May 1956, the *Ideal X*, a nondescript tanker, sailed into Houston harbour carrying a cargo that would change the world. The revolution did not come from the cargo itself but the way it was carried: the *Ideal X* was the first ship designed to carry cargo in containers, 58 of them.

In the following three decades containerisation became a highly automated system for shipping large quantities of freight at very low cost, seamlessly transferring loads to and from trucks, to railways and ships. That first journey hinted at the scale of the savings to come. In 1956 it would have cost about $5.80 per ton to carry a mixed load of loose cargo in barrels and sacks, pallets and crates on a medium-sized freighter. On the *Ideal X* the cost was 15.8 cents per ton.[76]

The man who put the *Ideal X* to sea, a maverick, ultra cost-conscious trucker called Malcolm McLean, was a frugal innovator: he started with an extreme constraint that was threatening his business. Congestion on the highway network meant his trucks often got held up in lengthy jams. Federal regulations meant he had few options to find different ways to transport his goods. Union rules meant he had to pay his drivers overtime. His business was slowly having the life squeezed out of it. McLean did not need to do market research; he was the first customer for his own innovation.

McLean wondered whether there was a congestion-free way to take goods to and from New York, by putting his trucks on boats. At the time this idea seemed impossible, technically and legally: competition law in the US meant that firms from the trucking industry could not enter the shipping industry. Not only was what McLean proposed unconventional and untested, it was also in all likelihood illegal. McLean only invented the container because he dared to ask for the apparently congestion-free freight transport.

McLean did not have an R & D lab, nor did he employ teams of designers. He did not engage in fundamental scientific research, nor did he employ design thinking and brainstorming techniques. Nothing about his innovation was glamorous or aspirational. First McLean did what most frugal innovators do: he borrowed – ideas and people; he rethought his way to a solution. He recruited Keith Tantlinger who had made the first modern 30ft aluminium containers that were stacked two high on barges operating between Seattle and Alaska. Tantlinger mocked-up the first containers in McLean's trucking yard. Then they found two huge disused cranes in a shipyard in Pennsylvania, cut them off at the legs and installed one in Newark and the other in Houston. The *Ideal X* was a worthless obsolete Second World War tanker which was refashioned to take Tantlinger's makeshift containers on its adapted deck. Tantlinger rigged up a do-it-yourself spreader that the crane operator attached to hooks on the container to lift it on and off. A single operator sitting 60ft above the ship could lower the spreader over a container, attach the hooks to the corners, lift the container onto the ship, release the hooks and start over. McLean did not have a budget for market research, nor for prototype testing. When regulators visited the yard to assess the containers' seaworthiness before their first voyage, they found McLean and Tantlinger jumping up and down on top of one.

McLean got the container revolution going because he had an extreme problem. To find a solution he challenged conventional wisdom and asked a seemingly stupid question: could goods be moved from trucks to ships and back again to avoid congestion? McLean's method was to recycle existing technology and infrastructure rather than building anything brand new: he adapted an obsolete tanker, cut up abandoned cranes and made and tested his own containers in his company's yard. The prototypes were developed in his trucking yard and tested in the real world, with real cargo. McLean and Tantlinger did not follow a grand design: instead they muddled through, solving problems as they went along and accepting that they would not find a solution to everything at once. They did not wait until they had a perfect product before launching; the *Ideal X* is what would now be called a minimum viable product.[77] McLean's assumption was that everything could be improved once the business was up and running.

McLean created the container, which is now ubiquitous and put to many uses, including for housing. Yet containerisation, the vast systems of ships, cranes and ports that today serve as the hubs of world trade, is what really changed the world. Containerisation changed the world because it became a system that was made by waves of innovators who followed in McLean's wake: of the 20 ports handling the largest numbers of containers in 2003, seven had seen little container traffic in 1990 and three had not even existed. Fifty years after the *Ideal X*'s revolutionary voyage the equivalent of 300 million 20ft containers were making their way across the world's oceans, with a quarter originating in China each year. McLean was a frugal innovator and the container was a frugal innovation: lean and simple, it dramatically reduced the costs and in its first incarnation, used by McLean, it had environmental benefits. Instead of each load sitting on a huge truck with its engine idling in heavy traffic, the containers shared a single ship, which never got stuck in traffic. Yet the frugal container eventually enabled the global explosion of industrial production and mass consumption that now threaten the planet's ecosystems. The container as a product, invented by McLean, was both frugal and low-cost. Containerisation as a system lowered the costs of trade and so brought many more places into the world economy, and so also probably helped to lift many millions out of poverty. Yet by allowing the dramatic expansion of trade, production and consumption the container has doubtful credentials environmentally. It is only a partially frugal solution.

In the future we will need more frugal innovators like McLean and Tantlinger, but it will not be enough for their innovations to be lean, simple and low-cost, because lower-cost innovations can just lead to a rebound effect of higher demand, more energy usage, more carbon, waste and pollution. We need frugal innovations that are lean *and* clean, while also being simple and social.

Frugal Systems

We need far more than frugal standalone products, the low-cost pumps and domestic water filters. We need complete frugal systems which create sustainable sources of water supply and encourage more thoughtful, careful approaches to consumption, from the two-minute shower in Queensland, Australia, to the Pepsee drip-irrigation system in India. These systems need to be cleaner in every sense, less energy-intensive and yet also more affordable for the millions who do not have access to clean water. The opportunity is even more obvious in energy: the world's poor already spend $31 billion a year on polluting, dirty forms of energy. Switching that consumption to cleaner, renewable forms of energy would be cheaper and cleaner. These new resource systems, especially for water and energy, have to be designed around natural cycles, to reuse, recycle, repurpose and remake as much as they can. Where innovation has been associated with the invention of the new, from scratch, using additional resources it will instead have to involve 're'-thinking – allowing us to make better use of what we already have. That means we will need new technologies that will simultaneously go forwards and backwards, to reinvent old-fashioned rain harvesting, market gardens, local cisterns, ponds and gasification plants in the era of the sprawling urban metropolis.

Clean is the third vital tool in the frugal innovator's tool box.

chapter 9

Social

The women look scared. Twenty of them sit in dejected silence on low benches in the lobby of the crumbling 1960s health centre on the edge of Mathare North, a Nairobi slum. They are staring blankly and in a state of shock. These women, all in the early stages of pregnancy, have just had what must seem to them a dreadful judgement delivered upon them. When they visited the health centre for what might be their first and only formal health check during their pregnancy a blood test revealed they were HIV+. The diagnosis would have sounded like a death knell. Most would imagine they would die as outcasts from their families, after being shunned and neglected, unable to protect their orphaned children. They looked defeated, desperate and haunted.

Yet thanks to remarkable advances in the treatment of HIV it is possible to deliver hope for these women through drugs that will prevent transmission of the virus to their babies; allow them to cope with the condition themselves and so extend their own lives by years. There is no reason anymore why being HIV+ should be a death sentence for mother or child. At least that is what has happened in the developed world, where rates of transmission for HIV from mother to child have fallen so steeply it is now virtually unheard of. Fewer than 7,000 pregnant women in the US each year are HIV+. In South Africa in 2009 that figure was 300,000.

South Africa, with 1 per cent of the world's population, has 17 per cent of the world's HIV infection. In Europe and the US roughly one child a day is born HIV+. In Africa it is 1,100. In South Africa 5.7 million people are living with HIV and there are 1.6 million AIDS orphans.

When Mitch Besser, an American HIV specialist, arrived in Cape Town in 2000 he was puzzled by why mothers would not take the drugs they needed to extend their own lives and save their babies from the virus. The solution at hand seemed so obvious and rational. Yet most women would almost go into hiding once they received their diagnosis. They would pretend for as long as possible they were not HIV+ to avoid the stigma that comes with the condition in societies where many still believe AIDS is caused by evil spirits. They would not come back to the health centre and avoid doing anything that would reveal their HIV+ status. Many would be isolated and fearful of how they might be treated by members of their own extended family. For more than two years Besser struggled to persuade expectant mothers newly diagnosed with HIV to return to his centre and start taking the drugs. Nothing worked.

The problem was that the health system lacked empathy; it treated the women's medical condition but was incapable of connecting to them as people. There were not enough nurses to talk women through their condition and how to cope with it. Sub-Saharan Africa has 24 per cent of the world's burden of the disease but only 3 per cent of the health workforce. South Africa is relatively well off by African standards: it has 408 nurses per 100,000 population. In the UK there are 1,200 nurses per 100,000. The lack of qualified healthcare professionals meant that when Besser arrived a nurse had to see more than 40 patients a day, for 12 minutes each. In those 12 minutes they had to counsel the woman on taking an HIV test; perform the test; dispense a dose of drugs; explain how to take them; go through options for feeding the baby and so on. There was no time to talk. The woman was then expected to walk out of the clinic, pick up her life and work out what to do. Not surprisingly many chose not to return.

Then almost by chance Besser noticed an older mother, who was already HIV+ and taking the drugs she needed to control the condition, counselling a younger mother newly diagnosed with HIV. That young mother continued coming back for more treatment because she had the support of an older mother to mentor her. Besser realised that mothers were far more likely to stick with the treatment programme if they were supported by another mother who was HIV+. The mentor mothers could talk about how to live with the stigma of HIV, confront the prejudice they would suffer and explain why it made sense to continue taking the drugs. They offered emotional support, practical tips and a kind of social know-how that was outside the remit of doctors and nurses. The medical system delivered advice and drugs to and for the women; the mentor mothers operated alongside them, working with them so they could cope with the condition by themselves.

Mothers-2-Mothers (M2M) formalised that 'with-and-by' approach and has taken it to scale. Mothers are recruited as mentors, given two weeks' training and a modest stipend to support them. Then they go to health centres to work alongside the nurses and doctors, providing social and emotional support. In Mathare the women have created a safe, warm and welcoming space, in which they talk openly about their condition and their lives and from seemingly meagre materials kindle a sense of hope and purpose. They radiate grace, honesty and tenacity. They are the secret weapon in the campaign against HIV.[78]

Working with a group of colleagues, some drawn from the US banking and entertainment industries, as well as a growing army of mothers and funding from the US government's Pepfor programme, M2M by 2010 was operating in 12 African countries and employing 1,500 trained mentor mothers who were seeing more than 230,000 pregnant mothers a month. In sites where M2M works it is common for the rate of mother-to-child transmission of HIV to have fallen from close to 90 per cent to less than 10 per cent. A fifth of all pregnant HIV+ mothers in the world are members of M2M.

The M2M solution is not medical or scientific but social: mothers working *with* one another. Doctors delivering a solution to the women were not effective on their own. The medical system, for all the knowledge it embodied, made little or no impact on the women because it did not connect with their lives. Medical knowledge about how to treat people became effective only when it was combined with the commitment of mothers supporting one another with the tacit knowledge of how to live with HIV. Systems that deliver products to and for people often need a social dimension to make a real connection. The most effective health solutions are invariably a mix of mutual self-help among patients combined with specialist systems delivering treatments for us. Providing that social dimension is often not costly but, like a pinch of spice in a curry, it provides the catalyst to bring the service to life. Nor does it take a genius to see how the social approach to frugal innovation could be combined with the lean production systems of the NH heart hospitals and the mobile platforms of MedicallHome to create a frugal health system.

We will need more recipes like M2M that work with people, in which people are participants in creating solutions rather than relying solely on professional systems to deliver goods and services for and to them. 'With' solutions are often more powerful, efficient, effective and innovative. They teach and spread through the power of peer networks and social influence rather than through top-down control and instruction. They are more flexible and adaptive and so they enable people to learn what works in the context they face. They mobilise additional resources and spread innovative ideas through word of mouth. Mitch Besser has pulled off an incredible trick: he has created a system that operates highly effectively, at low cost and great scale, but one which is capable of empathy, builds on relationships, respects intimacy and works with us rather than doing things to us.

Social Value

Much of what we most value we create together, with people, rather than having it delivered to us as consumers waiting to be served. These experiences are more like play and conversation: an interactive, shared, unfolding experience, not one programmed in advance. People programmed in advance to follow specific scripts are incapable of adaptation, imagination and empathy. That is why we often find systems so cold and impersonal. Mothers-2-Mothers is the very opposite: it bends to who you are because only then will it be able to help you take the drugs you need. You cannot deliver a solution to a mother with HIV the way that DHL delivers a parcel to your door. It may be efficient yet totally ineffective, because something vital will have gone missing: the social aspects of both the problem and its solution.

All of this gives us a different perspective from which to view the yawning gap between the systems we depend upon to make our lives efficient and the relationships that provide us with purpose and meaning. Love, friendship, intimacy, trust, care, respect, recognition and support cannot be selected from a catalogue, dragged and dropped into an online shopping basket, sold, packaged and shipped to you overnight. They are beyond price. These fundamental social goods, which make up much of what is most valuable in our lives, can only be created, with others, in often emotionally charged, pleasurable but uncertain activities, that involve a good deal of mutual accommodation, negotiation and improvisation. The dominance and narrow productivity of vast industrialised systems that do things for us means it has become easier for us to overlook and neglect the value of doing things with people.

Frugal systems, however, lack the heavy-duty resources of industrial systems – buildings, computers, hierarchies. That compels them to unlock mutual self-help as their main resource. Friendly systems like Mothers-2-Mothers are not just efficient in the narrow sense that they cope with a lot of people and deliver a lot of treatment; they are more effective in helping people to solve problems because they are socially productive, they reach parts of the problem that bureaucratic, professional systems do not reach. Cooperative solutions can reach further, at lower cost because they engage and mobilise people as contributors, not just consumers; they are capable of combining a capacity for intimacy and empathy, while also operating efficiently at scale. Frugal solutions like Pratham are highly relational: their lack of a traditional infrastructure means they have to scale through the relationships they create, which in turn brings in more resources.

All this means the social, our ability to make relationships, needs to be at the core of effective solutions in health, education and welfare. Relationships are at the heart of what makes for a good life. Living as a solitary individualist, for most people, is not a mark of success but a recipe for unhappiness. People grow up and age well if they have supportive relationships. Loneliness is reaching near epidemic proportions among older people in the developed world: more than 50 per cent of people over the age of 60 say they are lonely at least some of the time. The key to getting people to change their behaviour, whether that is to stop smoking, take up walking or start recycling their waste, is whether people they know and respect do the same thing. In any areas where lifestyle change is critical to public policy and corporate marketing, peer-to-peer networks will be vital. Relationships – what your friends are doing – change the way most people think and act.[79]

Relationships – what your friends are doing – change the way most people think and act

The recipes for mutual self-help being devised at scale out of necessity by frugal innovators like Pratham and M2M will be even more important in the future. The most effective systems in the future will support relationships, at scale, so people can find solutions with one another. They will be friendly, convivial systems.

This is why frugal innovators pose a direct challenge to some of the central tenets of mainstream economics, built on individualism and competition. The standard assumption in economics is that markets work best when they appeal to our individual self-interest. The baker and the butcher do not provide their bread and meat out of concern for our well-being but because that is how they make their own living. Yet frugal innovators connect with a daily life that also depends on a continual flow of reciprocal and unasked-for acts of kindness and consideration, often not mediated by money nor motivated by reward. Scientific evidence is mounting that we are as cooperative as we are competitive, inclined to be interested in the welfare of others, because we care about how they are treated and not just because we have a special connection to them or expect something in return.

Humans cooperate with strangers, not just our own kin. We form intimate bonds of friendship with people we are not genetically related to and make sacrifices on their behalf. We cooperate with people in one-off encounters even when there is no prospect of an act of kindness being reciprocated. We will even uphold norms of cooperation when there is no prospect of our earning a direct return simply because we believe such norms should be upheld.[80] Doing things together, with one another, does not go against the grain of our nature; it is written into who we are. Our evolutionary success depends on our ability for complex problem-solving, from how to hunt giant mammoth together to organising mass healthcare services, and complex problem-solving depends on cooperation. Frugal innovators help people come together to solve shared problems by tapping into these deep wellsprings of cooperation. Creative cooperation usually expands the ideas and resources we have, whereas competition often just divides up what we have. Cooperation can be *generative*: it creates more out of limited resources. That is why it is so central to frugal innovation.

Frugal innovators are turning these ideas about the value of cooperation into practical, everyday, low-cost solutions to basic needs. Sabis schools rely on high levels of self-governance and self-organisation among the pupils to take responsibility for non-curriculum parts of the school. Escuela Nueva has revolutionised learning in rural schools by promoting cooperative, self-organised learning among young children. Echale a tu Casa's brick machine is virtually useless unless an entire community unites to build houses together. The programme that Aziz Sagir has enrolled in at Esenler Merkez in Istanbul, the Mother and Child Education Programme, is a Turkish version of a programme first devised in Israel, which helps mothers to become first educators of their children. Mothers can be trained to support one another to ready their children for school. When it was launched in the 1980s the Mocep course lasted two years. Since then it has been made leaner and more focused. Almost 250,000 mothers, many of them illiterate, have been through the programme. Aziz says it has taught her how to pay more attention to her children, to help them rather than scold them, to see how she can help them in areas she might find hard herself. Long-term studies show that children who start school having gone through the Mocep programme are far more likely to complete secondary school and then go on to university. The programme has recently been enshrined in Turkish national education policy, making it available, in theory, to many millions of mothers. A small investment to help mothers help their families has had a huge multiplier effect: one facilitator can work with 25 mothers to help one another and it yields long-term benefits. In communities like Esenler Merkez where many people are recent arrivals from rural villages, social innovations like Mocep, a circle of mutual self-help, bring some of the collective, cooperative culture of the village into the heart of the city.

Frugal innovators excel at designing cooperative solutions. Where traditional companies see anything 'social' as a cost, an obligation or an unwanted constraint, frugal innovators see as their competitive advantage. It is how they get things done.

Make it Fun

When Suresh Kumar decided he wanted to create a service supporting people at the end of their life in the Indian state of Kerala, he quickly ran into an apparently insurmountable problem. Only a handful of doctors were trained in palliative care. Working out of a hospital they could at best hope to serve a few hundred people in one of India's most populous states. If Kumar wanted to reach everyone in Kerala he had to devise a different solution. Initially working in the Muslim villages in the north of the state he started to train volunteers to provide frontline care to families where someone was close to the end of their life. Now the Neighbourhood Network for Palliative Care (NNPC) has more than 10,000 trained volunteers who provide palliative care to more than 2,500 patients per week. The volunteers do not provide medical care, but if someone needs a doctor the volunteers know when and who to call. Instead they focus on the social and emotional challenges of people with chronic and incurable illnesses. As Kumar explained, they turn the challenge on its head: 'We see it as mainly a social challenge which has medical components, rather than seeing it as a medical issue which people need social support to cope with.'

The NNPC volunteers, who come from all walks of life and different age groups, help organise and provide personal care services, deliver medication, provide links to further social and spiritual support, as well as acting as the sensory system for medical services. Volunteers are encouraged to form local groups, identify end-of-life care needs and design appropriate supports, in contrast to a professionalised, top-down model organised around doctors. Almost no one dying in Kerala does so alone and without support. In the developed world end-of-life care is one of the most expensive and least satisfactory parts of costly and complex health systems. Yet Kerala has managed to create a highly effective system by redefining the challenge as a social one and by creating a dense mesh of volunteers to support people at very low cost.

Kumar and his team managed to recruit so many people because, he says, they made it fun to take part. When they go to a village to recruit volunteers they put on a small festival with food and music, they make a song and dance. Existing volunteers recruit people like them. People do it because their friends have signed up and because they like to be part of something bigger, to join a cause and to have a mission. None of that would have been possible if palliative care had been defined in purely professional, medical terms. The volunteers would have had nothing to contribute and no way to make their contribution. By recasting the challenge as social and creating a social movement to tackle it, Suresh Kumar found resources – willing and able volunteers – that traditional solutions would never have unlocked. Far from imposing a cost, the social mission of the service was vital to mobilise resources. *Having a social mission is a source of competitive advantage for frugal innovators.* Seeing people like yourself as part of the solution is another strength. That is why frugal innovators devise ways for consumers to share scarce resources. Social makes economic sense.

Collaborative Consumption

In the developing world shared access makes sense for a wide range of products that people cannot afford to own outright. Grameenphone's Village Phone service provides a villager with a micro credit loan to buy a phone which they can then rent out to other villagers per call or text. All of the village gets a phone, when they need it. The phone's owner is a Village Phone Operator. In the developed world, new kinds of shared solutions are emerging especially for hard-pressed urban consumers. The most established models are car sharing schemes such as Zipcar which allows consumers to rent a car just by the hour. Car club owners can pay for a car just when they are using it and they get a choice from a wide range of cars: if you need a larger car occasionally you can get one from the common pool. Many of the hassles of direct ownership are removed.

The shift towards shared, collaborative forms of consumption is only going to be accelerated by digital services which connect together not just ourselves but also millions of objects. Open source, free software, such as Linux and Drupal, are just two example of how shared solutions, frugal do-it-together solutions, can be both effective and low-cost and yet provide the basis for an entire economy of commercial applications. Wikipedia is an example of low-cost knowledge sharing, and the open courseware movement, started by MIT, of low-cost shared learning. These networks will make flexible, intelligent forms of sharing more possible. To date the most successful example is the website Airbnb, based on Couchsurfing, which allows people to rent out their spare rooms and even their own bedrooms when they are not being used. These are what commentator Lisa Gansky calls mesh solutions – sharing solutions enabled by networked technology, which connect lenders and borrowers of cars, tools, money, houses, bikes, land, books and much more. Some of these are trades for money; others involve barter and swaps. They all depend on people turning themselves from owners of idle consumer durables into micro-entrepreneurs, offering underused assets for rent. Seen as a whole, collaborative consumption offers leaner solutions: more of our assets are used more of the time by being shared.

All of this will become more acceptable with the spread of cloud computing when all our data – emails, documents, pictures, songs – will be stored remotely in a digital cloud hanging above us, always there for us to access from any device we like: computer, television, games console, handheld and mobile, embedded in our kitchen table, bathroom mirror or car dashboard. Shared services built on cloud computing should bring benefits for many millions of smaller organisations, which should be able to draw down from the cloud basic programs for customer relationship managing, online marketing, payroll, e-commerce, inventory management as and when they need them, expanding and contracting their capacity much more easily than it would if they had to own an IT infrastructure. In straitened circumstances young consumers are getting used to living 'hand-to-cloud': shared services make sense if they are lower-cost; don't own it unless you really have to; buy only as much as you need, when you need it.

Frugal innovators, both as consumers and producers, will drive these new forms of shared, low-cost solutions. A prime example of how both could come together is a remarkable collaborative platform created by a motley crew of independent music producers and festivals in Brazil called Fora do Eixo.

Free Culture

Fora do Eixo is an embassy of the future, at least that is how Felipe Altenfelder, one of its charismatic founders, likes to describe it. It is fair to say there is no embassy anywhere in the world quite like it. The creative heart of Fora do Eixo, what it officially calls its 'point of national articulation', is a sprawling, run-down detached house in an unfashionable suburb of São Paulo which even city natives struggle to find. There is no outward sign that this has become the epicentre of one of the most dynamic and disruptive forces in Brazilian popular culture and politics thanks to its own version of frugal innovation.

The interior of the house looks like the product of time travel, as if it has arrived from Berkeley in the 1960s: it's a sort of commune for the age of facebook. The team who work in São Paulo get somewhere free to live and food to eat in exchange for their labour. The walls are adorned with posters, graffiti art, abstract collages and antique paintings. Four people sit in one room intent on their computers tapping away, headphones on, working with makeshift tables and chairs. The kitchen is a bombsite. A few chocolate brownies scattered on a plate are the only food. A drink of water is delivered in a mug with a broken handle. No washing up seems to have been done for quite a while. A garage in the back yard has been converted into a performance space, where each Sunday a rock concert attracts about 400 people. The counter-cultural communes in Berkeley in the 1960s fed the cyber culture of the Internet more than 20 years later. The kids living and working together at Fora do Eixo are the heirs to that tradition but they are also taking it several steps forward. Like the original counter-cultural turned cyber utopians, epitomised by Stewart Brand, the founder of the Whole Earth Catalogue, they purvey an appealing mixture of hype and hope. Yet Fora do Eixo might have solved some of the fatal weaknesses that put paid to the communes of the 1960s as they collapsed in on themselves because they could not take hard decisions nor sustain themselves economically. Not only is Fora do Eixo quietly disciplined and hard-working, it has also created a sustainable, frugal economic model based on sharing.

Altenfelder is not necessarily an advertisement for the collective's success. He looks emaciated and wired, as ideas and slogans spill out of him in a dizzying whirl, as he waves his hands in front of him, blowing smoke from the thinnest of hand-rolled cigarettes. If Fora do Eixo is an embassy to the future then it's one that will alarm quite a few people and not just because the collective's main toilet is broken.

Fora do Eixo is an online platform, created and shared by an association of independent music festival producers all over Brazil so they can help one another put on events. In 2012 about 200 collectives in 27 Brazilian states were part of Fora do Eixo and together they put on almost 6,000 cultural events. Some of these events attracted thousands of people who drank vast quantities of beer and ate large amounts of food while they listened to bands both obscure and well known. Yet very little money changed hands to make all this possible. That is because Fora do Eixo has created its own parallel currency, the Cube Card, which is the basis of a trading system in which bands, producers, promoters, caterers, designers and many others trade favours with one another. The currency is carefully controlled to make sure it is not all spent on beer. In 2012 about 80 million Brazilian reals of trade was conducted on the Fora do Eixo platform: that was, $15 million in cash and the rest using the Cube Card. Altenfelder describes it as a way to systematise the brotherhood: not do-it-yourself but do-it-together. If a festival in Paraná in the south needs some help with some artwork, it might ask an artist associated with a collective in the far north-east to do the work. The credits the artist earns can be spent on some PR for his collective's festival, which might be done by someone working in São Paulo. People in the indie music business have long traded favours for one another. The Cube Card has simply systematised what was traditionally informal.

The currency in turn has introduced a discipline to the communes. Fora do Eixo is much more pragmatic that the pioneers in Berkeley. Indeed its members display what can only be described as a work ethic. When a client in the network agrees for a piece of work to be done by someone else, the task is logged on a Google spreadsheet, with the price, a description of the job, the person responsible and the deadline. The work is then tracked in the way that it would be by any project management software in a regular creative company. The producers are trusted to get the work done, much in the way of a self-organising work team. People who pay with their hard-earned credits expect something more than a favour; they want a decent service, to put on a professional show. Now the currency also embraces mainstream businesses outside Fora do Eixo, such as restaurants and bars. In exchange for advertising space and promotion at festivals, the bars provide credit which can be redeemed by people with the Cube Card.

Early in the platform's life Altenfelder and others realised that they would not get new members to use the platform's various tools, including the currency, unless they were trained to make it easy. So a Fora do Eixo University now runs about 180 courses a year to train people to use the platform. Nor is Fora do Eixo purist about using open source technology.

Instead they use whatever software tools are available, from Google and YouTube, to facebook and Twitter. Altenfelder says he will happily talk to Brazil's biggest companies – Petrobas is now a lead sponsor – as well as the most left-wing political parties. Quite soon it will become a broadcaster in its own right, using live streaming to relay its events. When people started travelling to festivals in large numbers they realised they needed their own accommodation service, a version of couchsurfing in which people offer their spare rooms and beds for free or rent. In 2012 more than 15,000 people found beds using the service.

Fora do Eixo defies easy categorisation. It operates a bank and a university; stages festivals and concerts; produces artwork and music. Yet at heart it is really a social movement of people committed to independent music. It is as much a social innovation as a technological and cultural one: it has created a recipe for people sharing their enjoyment of free culture. Fora do Eixo is deploying a Brazilian version of frugal innovation: the skills of *jeitinho*, to find a way to do something against the odds, and *gambiarra*, working within severe constraints to improvise something useful out of what is at hand, through sharing.[81] The skills of *jeitinho* and *gambiarra* were traditionally associated with the semi-legal practices of *favelas* and frowned upon in polite company. Now they are becoming an accepted part of more mainstream culture: what makes Brazil different, especially as it takes up the tools made available by the web and social media.

Think Like a Movement

This recipe has much wider application in a society in which some consumers are looking for something more meaningful in their lives than just owning the latest fashionable item. These experiences are invariably social, they bring people together: friends, families, lovers, fans and believers. That is also why we pay so much to be part of huge social gatherings despite the discomfort they often involve: festivals, carnivals, raves, sporting events, mass shows of emotion which give us a sense of being caught up in something more than ourselves by being with others.

Frugal innovators Suresh Kumar, Mitch Besser and Felipe Altenfelder have an instinctive sense of the appeal of being part of a social movement. The rewards are not just emotional. As Adam Smith pointed out in his *Theory of Moral Sentiments*, people do not just mechanistically calculate their self-interest; they are also concerned about how they are regarded by other people, their social standing. Regard cannot be bought and sold. Respect and recognition are earned by winning the approval of a community of peers. When frugal innovators build communities and social movements they give people the opportunity to earn the regard of their peers. People are mobilised to contribute by being part of something bigger. Creating shared, social experiences is not just about making better use of scarce resources; it can also mobilise and generate resources that were otherwise lacking.

Most mainstream businesses see anything social as an added responsibility: the cost of being seen to be a good corporate citizen might burnish their reputation but it does little to add real value to the business. In the conventional view, a business is no more than a means to an end. Whether that end is shareholder value, profit or return on equity, the point of traditional business is a financial measure of returns to the owners of the business. The main critique of this financially driven approach has come from the corporate social responsibility movement, which argues that companies need to take a wider and more responsible view of how they generate returns for shareholders. If a business is too callous or self-seeking then it attracts bad publicity; its reputation and public standing are damaged; that in turn corrodes its brand and undermines its value to shareholders. Being socially responsible is commercially expedient.

The organisations that frugal innovators create are social in a much deeper sense. They have a social sense of their obligations to and relationships with the people they serve. Being social is not an added, unwanted cost that the business has to bear, it is a source of competitive advantage. They create high-impact, low-cost solutions by being highly participative, cooperative and creating mutual gains for the organisation and the community it serves. They exploit their social advantage in six main ways.

The first social advantage is straightforward efficiency. The efficiency of the NH heart hospitals is partly driven by their sense of mission: to serve the poor. Many frugal innovators have hybrid business models like NH's, which charge some users fees to cross-subsidise a free service for those who cannot pay. The super efficiency with which the service is delivered creates the surplus which funds services for those who cannot pay. At NH social mission drives higher performance. The doctors want to do a better job because they have a social mission, not just to make money for the founder.

The second advantage is that social organisations create more effective ways for people to share scarce resources, making more of the few assets they have. These clever social solutions allow people to get more from limited resources through intelligent forms of sharing: clubs, mutuals, lending libraries, shared repositories of information and open source communities, attack the very high costs of individuals owning assets outright that they use only occasionally. In an era of more limited, constrained resources, shared solutions will become more important and so will organisations that have a social core to their constitution and mission.

The third social advantage is knowledge. Frugal innovators often create organisations that depend on high levels of peer-to-peer self-help. The basic unit of organisations like Mothers-2-Mothers and Mocep are circles of mothers which are multiplied into larger networks. Consumer self-help is not just low-cost, it can bring added advantages: the mentor mothers in M2M have a tacit, informal and social knowledge of how to cope with HIV that is unavailable to most professionals. They create better solutions because they act as translators between the medical system and the women they seek to help. Understanding the needs of consumers, seeing how a product or service fits into their lives, is one of the big challenges in innovation. It is all too easy for product innovators to make mistaken assumptions about how consumers will use their products. That is perhaps especially true when companies are dealing with unfamiliar and poorer consumers, who live in slums and *favelas*, sharing small spaces and lacking basic amenities. Traditional marketing techniques and distribution channels are too clumsy and cumbersome to reach into these communities. Frugal innovators pull off this trick by deploying their social advantage, using their position of trust within a community to get close to their consumers and gain added insight.

The fourth advantage is that organisations with a social purpose can mobilise additional resources. The mothers who attend Mocep's sessions are participants and collaborators, learning from one another, and in addition they are expected to be investors, putting in their own time and effort to deploy at home the skills they have learned together. Mocep works with its mothers and expects them to work by themselves in creating solutions that turn living rooms, kitchens and bedrooms in cramped apartments into little early years centres.

The fifth social advantage is the capacity to spread innovation. Frugal organisations spread innovation through word of mouth recommendation, imitation and emulation. In M2M, mentor mothers and their clients are the ambassadors for the programme, recruiting other mothers to the cause. When innovation involves behaviour change – as it invariably does in education, health, housing and environmental services – then organisations that can draw on strong social networks among consumers have an advantage. Time and again frugal innovations like the Pepsee and the Neighbourhood Network for Palliative Care spread at low cost through a process of peer-to-peer emulation which is written into their organisational DNA.

The final source of social advantage is that social movements often open up new markets, by challenging the status quo. Social entrepreneurs and frugal innovators are often trying to meet the needs of people who are overlooked by a distant political system and neglected by companies and markets because they are too poor and too hard to reach. As well as creating products and services that help people, they are necessarily engaged in a challenge to the political status quo and conventional wisdom. M2M is not just providing a service to mothers with HIV; it is also a campaign for their needs to be addressed. Mocep is not just a way for mothers to help one another. The organisation has led political debate in Turkey to get provision of early years education into the mainstream. The booming organic food market is the product of innovation in food production and retailing, which has been led by changes in consumer tastes, which themselves are products of a campaign that started in the margins of the industry 20 years earlier. Social movements highlight needs and so open up markets that were previously neglected. Organisations with a social sense do not just serve markets, they create them with the consumers they represent.

Frugal innovators derive profound advantages from their often cooperative forms of organisation. The pursuit of their social mission is a spur to be more efficient. Their ability to organise shared solutions allows them to make better use of scarce resources. By working closely and often employing people from the communities that they serve they get access to informal, tacit forms of knowledge which are highly valuable. Their ability to become social movements can mobilise additional resources and open up new markets. Their reliance on peer-to-peer networks helps them to spread innovations through word of mouth. The social advantage is the fourth and final ingredient in the frugal innovator's toolkit.

The Frugal Recipe

Frugal innovation creates better outcomes for more people, while using fewer resources, by developing completely different solutions.

At the core of frugal innovations are the four linked design principles: lean and simple, clean and social.

They are lean to eliminate waste in all forms. Lean thinking finds the most direct, efficient and elegant way to create what customers most value. It eliminates waste tied up in time-consuming bureaucracy, inflexible equipment and rigid systems. To be lean, frugal solutions also have to be simple.

Simple solutions can be used by more people, more easily. Complex products and technologies are more costly to develop, use and maintain. Simple solutions tend to be easier to use, more robust and easier to maintain. Simple solutions focus on the features that make most difference to consumers; look familiar, so they are easy to learn; and provide consumers with a complete solution, not just a fragment of one.

Innovations that are lean and simple can be low-cost without being frugal. To be fully frugal they also need to be clean: to minimise their environmental impact. Clean solutions rely on 're'-thinking: reuse, recycle, repurpose, remediate. They treat waste as fuel, use local renewable resources and are designed to work within natural systems.

Finally, frugal solutions make the most of being social to: engage consumers in adapting and innovating solutions; spread virally through word of mouth emulation and imitation; and share the costs among many people. Social, shared solutions will often be more economic than individualised, tailored ones. Frugal innovators work with the grain of cooperation to devise solutions with people.

These four design principles – lean and simple, clean and social – should be at the heart of innovation in the future. They are also central to how and where frugal innovation happens and who does it.

chapter 10

Who, How, Where?

Innovation is, often mistakenly, largely associated with a special breed of people – inventors, designers, researchers, boffins – working in special places – labs, design studios, creative quarters of cities – in special ways – often at odd hours, employing idiosyncratic forms of organisation. The implication is that to get more innovation we need more of these special people working in special ways in special places. The trouble is that these people are often creative because they are also detached from the real world, working in protected and artificial environments that are designed to allow them to think imaginatively. That often makes it difficult to translate their ideas into the real world. Much of what determines whether innovation is successful turns on this process of translation and adaptation: innovation is often more about how ideas are developed than it is about pure creativity.

Frugal innovation is often presented as an improvisational, grass-roots alternative to this formalised approach. The most famous expression of this do-it-yourself, makeshift approach is the Indian tradition of *jugaad* innovation and the Brazilian *jeitinho*: low-cost, practical and village-based innovation, which requires little formal knowledge. Grass-roots innovators improvise with whatever comes to hand, solving problems often at very small scale with few formal resources.

Both these approaches to innovation will lead us down a dead end if we pursue them exclusively. The kind of innovation we need in order to tackle the challenges we face lies in the combination of different kinds of knowledge, drawn from different disciplines and approaches. Formal, high-tech innovation, produced by the labs and design studios of the rich world, will be too detached from the realities and constraints of the lives lived by consumers in the developing world. Grass-roots innovation will be too patchy and improvisational to devise robust solutions that scale.

Innovation is an exciting, creative, daring activity. The new recipes that we create through innovation are how we generate more out of the limited resources at our disposal: it's a generative, creative process. That is why innovation is such an attractive, creative experience. However, innovation has a darker and more difficult side: it almost always involves deep and unsettling uncertainty and often outright conflict. That is because radical innovation often challenges the status quo and entrenched interests. As much as people are excited by the idea of innovation, they are deeply alarmed by the reality of how it shakes industries, upturns organisations, unsettles occupations, challenges assumptions and eliminates jobs. Promising innovations can tick all the right boxes and still fail because they incite the opposition of powerful interests who want to maintain the status quo, in which they have so much invested.

Frugal innovators often start with an advantage. They operate in extreme and marginal places where incumbents fear to tread. Their marginality means they have few resources. But it also gives them a latitude to adopt new approaches. As they are marginal they operate underneath the radar for quite a long time, not attracting much attention. If we look at who frugal innovators are, where they work and how they do it, then we will have a better idea of how to translate some of these techniques into larger, more established organisations.

Who

Frugal innovation is often associated with grass-roots, improvisational community-based problem solvers conjuring solutions from the meagre materials they have around them, turning a tube for iced water into a drip-irrigation system and vacant urban plots into a city's food supply system. They have limited theoretical knowledge but a deep and intense knowledge of the people they are serving and where to find local resources, because they come from those communities themselves. They have no need for expensive and specialist ethnographic research. Often they do not have labs or studios to experiment in; they have no option but to experiment, continually in the real world, with real people and products. They learn in action, not through theory. Their weaknesses mirror their strengths. Their knowledge and resources are limited to the localities in which they operate. Their innovations often fail to spread and scale; they get trapped on location. They may miss opportunities to apply technologies evident to people with more formal training and skills.

All successful frugal innovation depends upon the embrace of this localised knowledge and insight, to get close to where the problem is, understand what resources are available in situ and how a solution will fit into people's lives. But these grass-roots innovators are just one source of inspiration for frugal innovation.

Another quite different group has also provided a stream of frugal innovation: the research and development labs of multinational companies exploring commercial opportunities at the bottom of the pyramid. Increasingly these labs are located in the markets where the products are sold and staffed by local researchers. These research centres in Bangalore and Shanghai often have quite a distinctive feel: they are more about development than pure research. The people in them are highly productive and not afraid to borrow, mix and blend ideas from elsewhere in the pragmatic search for better solutions. They bring highly theoretical and developed knowledge to bear on practical problems. That is how staff at GE's centre in Bangalore came up with a super low-cost ECG machine with its printer borrowed from the bus station and how Tata came up with the Swach, which blends the latest nano materials with local materials to filter water. Multinationals bring with them an understanding of how to run lean production plants and scale distribution to very large markets using familiar brands.

A third group of frugal innovators are socially responsible designers and researchers, often based in the US, Europe and Australia, who deploy highly theoretical knowledge, in quite specialised environments, to unpick the science and design of frugal solutions. These designers and researchers, the likes of the team at Monash University who came up with the aerosol to deliver oxytocin for mothers, employ much more formal processes to arrive at a more theoretical informed understanding of a solution. Designers play a particularly important role in understanding how solutions can be made functional, elegant and appealing, so frugal innovation does not appear to be second best. They stand at the other end of the spectrum from grass-roots, improvisational innovators who rely on tacit knowledge to create practical solutions that work.

The final significant group are the entrepreneurs who are creating the business and organisational models needed to make frugal innovation flourish. One part of this is business model innovation to create new ways for poorer consumers with unpredictable finances to afford products and services. A frugal innovation that works, technically, but which poorer consumers cannot afford to buy will be stillborn. That is why frugal innovators often have to help create the market their innovations serve. Echale a tu Casa does not just provide communities with a brick-making machine – it also helps them to plan their building programme and organise the finance. Naandi's water treatment plants work not just because of the technology but because they have adopted a pay-as-you-go card system familiar to mobile phone users. The NH heart hospitals meet their social mission, which motivates their staff and partners, by operating a hybrid model in which richer patients in effect cross-subsidise services for the poor.

These entrepreneurs are also organisational innovators, which allows them to reach a lot of people at very low cost, without going through the normal channels of mass market distribution. Frugal innovators have no option but to adopt organisational forms considered unusual by big business. Often they are a mixture of organisations, movements and platforms for self-help. Frugal innovators like Pratham and M2M are creating 'radicant' organisations: they put down roots, draw in and create the resources to sustain themselves as they grow. The NH heart hospitals are disruptive because they apply principles honed in factories and vast retail stores to the job of providing healthcare. Often these entrepreneurs are regarded as heretics by the mainstream professionals.

Frugal innovation comes from how the knowledge of all these different people is brought together in the most creative way. Frugal innovation does not come from a single individual but from teams and collectives, often working together over long distances, but focused on a particular problem or market opportunity. Frugal innovators are the people who stand at the point where all this comes together. They have a special ability to see how diverse kinds of knowledge can be combined, to solve problems in difficult circumstances. They rarely work all their time in the ivory tower of academia but they respect how scientific researchers can contribute insights unavailable in the village and the slum. They do not have the resources of a large multinational company, but they respect what can be learned from large organisations that deliver high quality and high productivity. They may not come from the villages and slums where solutions are needed, but they understand these places and respect the tacit knowledge, ingenuity and resourcefulness of the people who live there.

Frugal innovators must be inquisitive, open-minded and interested in an eclectic range of ideas and know-how. They do not confine themselves to a single domain of knowledge. They respect theoretical knowledge but above all they are practical, pragmatic problem solvers. Often, like Devi Shetty at the NH heart hospitals, they are missionary-innovators, driven by a moral cause and a sense of calling to make a difference. They are visionary but not lost in the clouds: they are deeply pragmatic about how to get things done in the real world.

Most important of all they tend to be both rooted and yet cosmopolitan. They are rooted in the knowledge and concern they have for the people and places they are helping. They see the people they work with not as dependent and needy but as bearers of rights and aspirations, equipped with know-how and ideas that will help them to enact solutions themselves. But at the same time as being deeply rooted and committed to the places where they work, they are highly cosmopolitan: they connect internationally with other people, ideas and insights, which they bring back to these places. That helps them open up local problems to a wider set of solutions. That combination – rooted and cosmopolitan – runs through most successful frugal innovation. The NH heart hospitals were the brainchild of a consultant who grew up in India, trained in the UK and drew on techniques from McDonald's and Walmart to create low-cost heart surgery. Suresh Kumar, the inspiration behind the Neighbourhood Network for Palliative Care, trained as a palliative care specialist outside India before returning to Kerala. The Mother and Child Education Programme in Turkey developed from a programme created in Israel that the founders learned about while studying in Britain. Gyanesh Pandey created Husk Power Systems after returning to India from working in electricity supply in the US. Mothers-2-Mothers was the creation of an American HIV specialist working with mentor mothers in the townships of South Africa.

Frugal innovation thrives when people working with extreme constraints challenge conventional wisdom, ask impossible questions and then create new combinations of ideas drawn from a mix of the local and the cosmopolitan. The answers to the challenges we face will not be found in either the research labs of universities in the West or in the slums of the developing world, but in how ideas from both are brought together. That in turn means that perhaps the most important policy to promote frugal innovation in future will be to encourage the circulation and combination of people and ideas, from North and South, research labs and slums, big companies and micro-markets. Circular migration of talent around the world is probably the single most important factor in frugal innovation.[82] That also explains where we should look to see where frugal innovation happens.

Where

To understand what frugal innovation is you have to see where it happens. Frugal innovation thrives in particular places which are not the usual locations for innovation.

The conventional account of formal scientific and technical innovation is that it happens in special places, where innovative people can work in special ways: labs, design studios, innovation zones, which outwardly declare what makes them especially innovative. Sometimes in big companies one will find 'innovation zones' that usually contain some bean bags, a cappuccino machine, table football, brightly coloured walls (favourites include lime green and orange) and Lego bricks. The fundamental design principle of these special innovation zones is that creativity will emerge from them because they lift the normal constraints that people work under and which hold back their imagination. Lifting the constraints of humdrum surroundings and bureaucratic procedures helps people to become creative. Creativity is associated with freedom from constraints.

Often it seems as if there is no one inside these spaces because they are artificial, contrived and pre-programmed. They stand as architectural symbols of creativity, a way to project the idea of innovation. In proclaiming their creativity they often kill it off because creativity thrives in places where people feel relaxed and uninhibited, where conversation flows easily. Innovation often thrives in the places that look the least innovative (kitchens, garages, backyards, bedrooms). The places also need to encourage open, easy communication so new ideas can spread among different people. They are also open to the world so people constantly bring new ideas into the mix. They provide people with the time, permission and resources to try out ideas and get rapid, helpful feedback on their development. Many of the places where innovation is officially meant to take place look shiny and new. They often feel rather cold and dead, neither playful nor intense, neither convivial nor collaborative.

Frugal innovation usually involves combining many different kinds of knowledge, from researchers and designers, as well as engineers, consumers and entrepreneurs, and so it has to be drawn from the many different places where these people work. Global philanthropists such as the Gates Foundation and social impact funds such as Acumen are starting to convene the networks where these ideas converge, particularly around big social and health challenges such as saving the lives of mothers and babies at birth. Digital platforms and networks, such as Kiva, are helping to connect entrepreneurs and innovators in the developing world to investors in the developed world.

But the most important places for frugal innovation will be where these ideas are most needed. Frugal innovation comes to life in places that are completely different from special, self-conscious zones of innovation in the developed world. Frugal innovation thrives when people experiment in the real world rather than apart from it. Frugal creativity thrives because of constraints. Rather than excluding ordinary, real people, in favour of people with special skills of creativity, the places where frugal innovation thrives embrace practitioners and consumers as part of the process. Their knowledge of how to make things work in practice and to solve practical problems in applying an innovation is essential. The places for frugal innovation are thus usually marginal, unassuming places. When McLean and Tantlinger invented the container they were not part of an innovation programme, they were simply trying to solve a difficult problem. Madhav Chavan did not create the idea of Pratham, he borrowed and then developed it, rapidly in the real world, with barely literate women.

Frugal innovators are both rooted and yet cosmopolitan: so the places where they will thrive are likely to be cities, especially in the developing world, where they can simultaneously be close to the consumers who need their innovations and yet easily connect to international flows of ideas, talent and money. The most cosmopolitan cities of the developing world that benefit from circular flows of migration, with talented and entrepreneurial people returning with ideas and connections from the knowledge centres of the developed world, will be the most potent sources of frugal innovation in the future. These are the places where the battle for our future will be won and lost. The best ideas of the 21st century will come from the people who live, work and congregate in these cosmopolitan cities in the developing world. There is no better example than the city of Curitiba in Brazil – arguably the leading frugal city in the southern hemisphere.

The Micro-Recyclers

Rodrigo Muscolevy is tired. For eight hours he has been tramping the streets of Curitiba, a city in central Brazil, pulling his makeshift, light green, handmade cart called 'Interprise II' behind him, collecting rubbish to be recycled. On a good day, after two or three outings, Rodrigo can collect enough to earn about £5 when he delivers his load to the recycling centre. Today his cart is full with 80kg of plastic, glass and metal and he should earn about £2.50. Rodrigo is one of a small army of recycling entrepreneurs created by a remarkable example of mass social innovation, orchestrated by Curitiba's city council, which has turned the city into a centre for frugal innovation.

Curitiba has not innovated a standalone service or product but an entire system for producing a public good: a cleaner, more environmentally sustainable city. Curitiba has charted the emergence of an entirely new system for dealing with waste which is simultaneously lean and simple, social and clean. It is lean because it minimises waste in all forms: household waste is collected and recycled efficiently using minimal resources thanks to micro-entrepreneurs such as Rodrigo. In Curitiba they call it rubbish that is not rubbish. It is simple because someone like Rodrigo can start a recycling business from scratch, with no training and little capital. All he needs is a rough and ready handcart. It is social because the city gets a better shared solution to its waste challenge and it is clean because Curitiba manages to recycle more waste than cities its size in the developed world. The army of micro-recycling entrepreneurs in the city is a radicant form of organisation: as the city grows so does the need for recycling but so do the business opportunities.

Curitiba's challenge, like many cities in the developing world, is to encourage order to emerge from the ever-present threat of chaos. Each year between 20,000 and 30,000 people come to the city from the countryside looking for a better life. Often they have no education, trade, skills, place to live nor sense of what it means to be a citizen of a city. All over town, but particularly along riverbanks and under power lines, migrants throw up shanties which spread like a forest fire as word spreads that a new area of land has been invaded. It takes just a few weeks for a field to become a *favela* housing thousands of people. Curitiba's response has been a kind of frugal, structured self-organisation.

The most striking example of this philosophy in action is Cujaru, a former squatter encampment on the city's edge which houses thousands of people on land that was pasture in 1990. As the Cujaru settlement grew the city got a loan from the Inter American Development Bank to replace the *favela's* shacks with permanent houses. The bank stipulated that the council had to contract with a registered builder to build the new homes. Pretty soon builders were throwing up standardised, low-rise housing units that looked rather like army barracks. The city council called a halt and went back to the bank with a proposal for a different approach.

The contractor's houses cost $10,000 per unit. The council argued that if people were allowed to pursue frugal solutions, to build their own houses, employing their own labour – often family and friends – the cost would be about $3,000. Instead of the area being blanketed by one-size-fits-all barrack-style housing, Cujaru would have a variety of architectural styles. People who build their own homes would look after them and their neighbourhood, the council pointed out. If something went wrong with the plumbing, for example, the householder would fix it themselves rather than turning to the council to provide a solution. Eventually the council persuaded the bank that its frugal approach would be far more cost-effective: people would be participants in the process rather than recipients of a top-down service. In the first four months of the revised scheme 10,000 homes were self-built and Cujaru is now a thriving, stable community of thousands of self-build homeowners.

Curitiba practises frugal innovation as a city. As a result it is both more economically successful than many other cities – because it has low-cost systems – but also more sustainable. Curitiba is one of the most cosmopolitan of Brazilian cities, with large migrant populations drawn from Japan, Italy and the Baltic States. This mix, and the connections it makes to the wider world, are a critical part of what makes the city so successful.

It has also managed to combine the formal knowledge of engineers and architects with the improvisational innovation of entrepreneurs. Many of the city's strategies, including its ultra low-cost bus-based public transport system, were devised by Curitiba's Institute of Public Policy (IPPUC). It was IPPUC engineers who designed the revolutionary roll-on roll-off system for boarding buses that is at the heart of Curitiba's mass transport system. That is because 2,530 buses make 21,000 journeys a day to carry 2 million passengers, along 71km of bus-only lanes within the city and more than 270km of feeder routes. More people travel by bus in Curitiba than in New York City. The busiest interchanges at the edge of the city handle 35,000 passengers an hour. However, it's not just the institutions and skills of leadership that count, but their style and ethos. Since the 1970s Curitiba's political leaders have mainly been non-politicians. Jaime Lerner trained as an architect; Cassio Taniguchi was one of Brazil's top engineers. Both brought to their office a pragmatic, technocratic, problem-solving style. Their charisma comes from being quiet and thoughtful. That non-egotistical style of leadership is vital if innovation is to draw out contributions from many different people.

Curitiba is an outstanding example of a city as a breeding ground for frugal innovation: a city that is social, lean and green. High in the mountains of Paraná it has a distinctive culture and feel. Yet it is highly cosmopolitan, with large populations with cultural and family ties to Europe and only an hour's flight from São Paulo. If you want to find the frugal innovators of the future, go to cities like Curitiba, places which are inventive and ingenious, rooted and cosmopolitan.

How

Innovation cannot be delivered the way that Domino's delivers a pizza. There is little point in instructing people to have new ideas, just in time, according to a detailed production schedule. It is impossible to specify in detail in advance the outcomes of innovation; if that were possible it would not be innovation. As a result innovation is hard to manage in a traditional way precisely because it involves so much uncertainty and risk, trial and error, experimentation and learning, adaptation and reinterpretation.

Yet despite the unavoidable uncertainty associated with innovation, which makes it difficult to know in advance quite what might go wrong and what new ideas might emerge, innovation does involve a common set of activities: sensing, responding and acting; thinking, playing and making. Frugal innovators approach these activities in a particular way. They have their own methods.

At its most basic innovation involves three core activities:

- sensing, which means looking outward, for threats, challenges, changes in the environment, opportunities and needs, macro and micro;
- responding, which involves analysing, interpreting what has been found out and formulating initial responses, concepts, ideas and turning them into prototypes and products;
- acting, which involves turning ideas into products and services, testing and refining, developing and eventually scaling.

Sensing is about listening, observing, learning, withholding judgement, being prepared to jettison assumptions and adopt new vantage points, however uncomfortable and uncertain that might be. Responding is generative and problem-solving and it often involves the combination of previously separate ingredients, often in real time, with consumers. Combination and recombination are at the heart of almost all innovation. Acting is about making things happen in the real world. Innovators like turning ideas into real products and services. Creativity is not the only nor the most important skill involved in innovation; being able to develop and then scale a product or service is absolutely vital. Many innovations fail not because they do not work but because what works does not scale and what scales cannot be sustained as a business.

These three core activities are iterative and cyclical, rather than linear and consequential. Acting is not just the end of the process but also its start. By acting in the world, innovators test out ideas and sense how they need to be refined. Innovation can fail at any point in this cycle. Often innovators fail because what appeared to be a good solution failed to really address the needs of their consumers. Even if an innovation works and it is clearly needed, it may not be adopted by consumers (e.g. AIDS treatments in Africa which come with a social stigma). The mobile phone that took off as a consumer product when a new business model – pay-as-you-go – made it available to a mass market. Business model innovation and changes to consumer behaviour are often as important as the product innovation itself. Innovators have to be adept at pivoting and pirouetting to look in new directions for solutions. Those twists and turns often lead to new partnerships and alliances.

Managing that process of combination, exploration and discovery is the core skill of innovation. Innovation requires divergent, imaginative, free-thinking some of the time, especially when new ideas are being generated, followed by periods of convergent, disciplined thinking when the most promising ideas have to be selected for further development. Most innovation depends on small, tight-knit teams who work together very intensively, in their own small world. But at critical points those teams also have to be open to the wider world, to gain ideas and test prototypes, often through co-development with partners and consumers. Innovative organisations move easily between these different modes of work: they respect the need to be disciplined and focused as well as open and creative; they engage people who have bold ideas but also people who thrive on making things happen in the real world.

There is no single recipe for how frugal innovators work. They draw on many different approaches. Socially responsible designers bring techniques of ethnography, user research, prototyping and visualisation and design thinking. Researchers in multinational companies are able to bring skills used to make and market solutions that work at scale. Grass-roots, social entrepreneurs have an instinctive, sense of how improvisational solutions can be assembled to fit into people's lives. Yet underlying these different approaches to innovation are common rules of thumb, approaches that all frugal innovation shares. Frugal innovation is rarely a neatly structured process of consumer insight, research, design and prototyping, and more a real world process of trial, error and adjustment, to improve an initially imperfect but viable product.

Frugal innovators follow eight rules of thumb:

Get real

Frugal innovators work in the real world in which their innovations will have to work, rather than in artificial, well-resourced and contrived environments cut off from the world. At some point in the process frugal innovators retreat and reflect in a lab or a studio, to look for new ways forward. But the true test of an innovation is whether it works in the real world and so frugal innovators seek to get real as fast as possible. That reduces the risk that they might devise a prototype that looks attractive in the studio but fails in the real world.

Design, but don't overdesign

Designers can find the most elegant and simple way to make a product pleasing and functional. Consumers do not want second-best, hand-me-down products. They want products that are well designed to fit into their lives, and which give them effective solutions. Yet design can be the enemy of effectiveness when it becomes an end in itself, a testimony to the skills and creativity of the designer. Overdesigned products can be too costly and complex to work in the tight conditions faced by most emerging world consumers. Frugal innovation depends on designers who follow Naoto Fukasawa's philosophy, to find the simplest, most elegant, least invasive way to provide a solution that draws out the intelligence and skills of users. Frugal innovators do not seek shiny, sleek perfection.

Stay close

Understanding the lives of consumers, how they will adapt a product and what else they need to complement it are also vital. In formal design and innovation processes this insight is often provided by market research, focus groups and ethnographic studies. One of the reasons frugal innovators tend to do their innovating in the real world, is that they get to work with real consumers, first hand in real time, to develop more effective solutions. They seek to understand not just how their product will be used but how their consumers live their lives and the pressures, constraints, assets and possibilities available to them. A good example is Patrimonia Hoy, a Mexican subsidiary of the cement company Cemex, which provides small packets of cement to people in slums who are building their own homes. This is a radical departure from Cemex's traditional, core business model whereby it sells very large quantities of cement wholesale to big construction companies and building materials distributors. The idea behind Patrimonia Hoy is to tap into a very large, new market, in which a long tail of self-builders buy very small quantities of cement. To make Patrimonia Hoy work, the company needed to develop a close relationship for the first time with its ultimate consumers: homebuilders. Quite soon Patrimonia Hoy realised that selling self-builders small packets of cement was the easy part. To use the cement effectively self-builders needed advice from architects and most importantly help with their finances, which were often highly variable. According to Israel Moreno, the founding chief executive of Patrimonia Hoy, it is usually the women in the family who drive the big decisions about needing a better house. Most want more space to accommodate children. Some want to rent out rooms, almost like a pension. Others want to accommodate their poor parents.

Frugal innovators cannot afford lengthy design processes which involve only episodic engagement with their consumers. They have to be embedded in the communities they serve and use agile development processes, in which they rapidly develop and iterate their designs.

Borrow

Rapid, real world learning encourages innovators to borrow from existing, proven approaches rather than inventing from scratch. Frugal innovators reuse and recycle because it is a more efficient and effective way to learn. They prefer to piggyback on existing infrastructures rather than investing in their own. They adapt and incorporate products and solutions that other innovators have already developed. Innovation is not always about forecasting and projecting into the future: looking ahead. Frugal innovators learn to look sideways for those ideas (to import a bus station printer into a medical device, for instance), and they look backwards (to recover simple, effective ideas which have been discarded prematurely). Frugal innovators never assume they are working from a blank sheet, nor that all previous attempts to solve the same problem have been a failure. That means they are willing to recognise the ideas and contributions of others. That in turn means they tend not to be heroic and arrogant but humble and unassuming: they see borrowing from others as a sensible strategy.

Make allies, share value

Successful innovation is rarely just about creating a standalone product. Echale a tu Casa's brick-maker does not require many inputs other than the labour of the villagers and local dirt. But to make the bricks useful the villagers need to plan how they will build their houses and how they will pay for them. The innovative brick machine needs complementary services, such as architects and financial services to organise the finance. Successful innovation usually involves bringing together contributions from several different players and that means innovators need to build alliances around their products by sharing some of the value that gets created with the other members of the alliance.

Successful innovation involves bringing contributions from different players

Complementary assets, products and services are often essential to bring out a product's full potential. Edison's lightbulb beat the competition in part because he realised it would be useless without a means to generate and distribute electricity. Edison innovated a complementary set of technologies, not just a standalone product.

Frugal innovators often say they are leading movements, not just organisations. That is because they recognise that their innovations depend on alliances of partners, developers, distributors and consumers. Radicant organisations like Pratham are alliances made up of many small cells. When women are recruited and trained to set up a new *balwadi*, they are brought into the movement and become part of the alliance. Frugal innovators lack resources, so they have to be adept at drawing together resources from others around them.

Stay flexible

Frugal innovators have to be able to look for different ways forward when they hit an obstacle. They are pragmatic, unafraid to take a detour to reach their destination. Eric Ries in *The Lean Startup* calls this pivoting.

To 'pivot' you need to be focused on the consumers and the need you are trying to satisfy rather than the specific product or service you are providing. You need to be unsentimental and ready to cast aside elements that do not work, even if their original designers are very attached to them. Pivoting means being able to stand back with a certain detachment from your own invention and to see its weaknesses. The obstacles to success might be: technical (the kit might not work because it's too heavy, fragile, complex, costly, unfamiliar); social (consumers might not be willing and able to fit the new product into their lives, to see its value to them); business-related (even if the product works and it is liked by consumers it may still prove impossible to get it to market and make money from it). More often than not, pivoting entails looking for a different way to engage consumers and create a business model. It requires not just innovation but entrepreneurship, to seek new ways to create a viable business. Mitch Besser at M2M had to pivot when he finally understood that his mainly medical approach to persuading HIV+ mothers to take anti-retroviral drugs was less effective than an approach which enlisted mothers' know-how and support. MedicallHome started as a premium rate telephone line, which consumers paid for by the minute and almost failed before it pivoted to become a mobile phone-based service, in which consumers paid through their mobile phone subscriptions. Now it is pivoting again to become a marketplace for primary healthcare services. Suresh Kumar initially wanted to create a traditional palliative care service with trained doctors and nurses. When he realised this would be impossible he pivoted to create a mass movement of volunteers to create the service's front line. Frugal innovators excel at pivoting.

Creative muddling through

In 1959 the political scientist Charles Lindblom, in a brilliant paper called *The Science of Muddling Through*, argued that in complex, shifting, uncertain environments it was impossible to know and plan everything in advance, through analysis and rational planning. Instead, he said, in those situations managers had to learn the art of 'skilful incompleteness' when they had to muddle through creatively, adapting and adjusting to changing circumstances without knowing all the possible outcomes. Lindblom argued this skill meant being able to focus on problems they could define while leaving other, more difficult, opaque challenges, unaddressed. Creative muddling through relies on a high tolerance of ambiguity; a clear sense of priority to use scarce resources most effectively; an acceptance that not everything is always going to be under control; a willingness to sort things out later if necessary. Slums are complex, shifting and uncertain environments: muddling through is the method that works best there. Frugal innovators such as Madhav Chavan, the leader of Pratham, is a pre-eminent exponent of the art of creative muddling through, improvising and improving on a solution which started out only just good enough.

Thrive on constraints, use crisis to be creative

Frugal innovators use constraints to work in their favour. More than that, they use crisis creatively to unlock new solutions by enabling new thinking, making people drop ingrained habits and forcing a sense of urgency. Time and again frugal innovators have used crisis as a turning point to get people around them to accept the need for unconventional thinking and ideas. Toyota's lean production system came into life when the company faced a crisis which threatened its future. Havana invented its system of urban agriculture when it could no longer afford to import food. Singapore created its system of urban reservoirs to catch rain and started to recycle water when shortages threatened its future. Sabis had to invent new techniques for teaching when it spread from the Lebanon in response to the civil war. Each time crisis was the spur to a new solution. Frugal innovators respond to crises not by battening down the hatches, but by realising they mean the world needs to be seen in a different way.

chapter 11

In Reverse

The biggest challenges we face, in terms of the scale and speed at which we need to innovate, are to create new systems for water, energy, housing, health and education in the fast-growing cities of the developing world. The most painful challenge we face, however, may be in the developed world, to remake the established, incumbent, high-cost, highly engineered, specialist systems, products and services on which we have come to rely. Re-engineering and replacing those systems and products so they are more affordable and environmentally sustainable will involve not just creating new solutions – risky enough – but challenging and dislodging existing solutions. That challenge will provoke conflict. Innovation is creative, generative and exciting. But in the developed world, at least, it will also be seen as threatening, unsettling and destructive. Innovation will go hand in hand with conflict as well as creativity. Successful companies, cities and public services will not turn away from these conflicts. Nor will they minimise what is at stake. They will know how to respond creatively to the challenge. A prime example of the kind of leadership this will involve comes from the automotive industry, for so long the source of American and European leadership in industrial innovation.

Rethinking the Car Radio

The software and information components of cars are increasingly important, from the programs that control the engine and brakes, to entertainment, navigation and communication systems people rely upon. For some consumers the most important part of a car is the radio. Younger consumers increasingly see cars through the lens of social media: a car is a tool to maintain social connections and they want to stay connected whilst driving. All of this means that the infotainment and communications systems that cars use are increasingly important.

The top end of these systems has long been dominated by the German company Harman, created in 1953, which supplies the likes of BMW, Audi and Mercedes-Benz.[83] Harman, like so many high-end German engineering companies, has an enviable position in the luxury end of the market. As many companies of its ilk in Germany, Harman is dominated by engineers who are proud of their specialist knowledge and exacting standards. To stay ahead of the competition in the high end of the car market these engineering aristocrats tend to design ever more advanced, sophisticated systems, incorporating a wider range of features.

When Dinesh Paliwal was made chief executive in 2007, however, it was with a mandate to tap the fast-growing markets of China and India. Initially Harman tried to sell scaled-down versions of its high-end German products. These second-best solutions did not go down well. Paliwal realised that finding new customers in much more price-sensitive markets would mean creating new products with them in mind. Sachin Lawande, then Harman's chief software architect, was charged with the project to create these breakthrough products, code named Saras, which in Sanskrit means adaptable and flexible.

One might think that a project designed to tap into the fastest-growing consumer markets in the world might be met with excitement and enthusiasm. Far from it. Saras was first greeted with indifference, suspicion, scepticism and eventually outright hostility as it gained momentum. The more serious Lawande got, the more opposition the project provoked. The project was seen as an affront to Harman's tradition, the products of which would cannibalise its higher-end products. For engineers lower cost signalled lower quality, lower status and less rewarding jobs. Eventually, however, Lawande and his team succeeded. As a result Harman has a range of products both for the higher end of the market and the lower end. More European and US companies, hospitals and schools will need this capacity to look both ways at the same time. This is how he did it.

Lawande started by setting a stretching goal. Harman's engineers had been used to being able to build greater complexity and cost into their products. Lawande insisted the Saras infotainment system had to be half the price of its traditional systems and a third of the cost. Meeting that cost constraint meant rethinking what products did, how they were built and how they were designed. Every aspect of conventional wisdom at Harman needed to be challenged.

The Saras team quickly realised they would need to focus on the main features that customers needed, as opposed to those the engineers and designers thought they should have. That meant eliminating many higher-end features and focusing on those things people used 80 per cent of the time: the radio, the sat nav and the phone. To drive down costs Lawande insisted Harman should start using open source software rather than in-house developers and adopt modular designs for components that could easily be reused in different settings. Rather than designing custom-made chips – a distinctive mark of high quality in an Audi – they started adapting mass market chips that were widely used in smartphones. Making all this work required significant changes to how Harman operated. Lawande insisted teams became less specialised and hierarchical and more collaborative and generalist in their skills and outlook. Traditionally engineers had focused on their area of expertise and the components they were responsible for. In Saras they were encouraged to work collaboratively to better meet the needs of their customers, for communication, entertainment and mapping. The design teams were organised into a series of rapid sprints, short development projects that lasted no more than a couple of weeks, so they got rapid feedback. Traditionally new product development was a lengthy, complex business in which all the parts were interrelated. Lawande made the process much simpler and sharper.

The consequence was that Saras created a product with higher profit margins than the higher-end products, despite the much lower price, which opened up vast new markets because it could be installed in mass market, mid-priced cars. In 2011, about 18 months after launch, the new systems had generated about $3 billion worth of sales. The Saras infotainment is a frugal product: it is simple in design; developed through a lean process; uses shared, open source software and reuses existing technologies.

Most importantly, although Harman shifted the centre of gravity for this project to India and China, it pulled it off with Harman engineers. It turned them into rooted cosmopolitans. It took them into the market they were designing for but asked them to bring the skills and knowledge that had made them so successful, to apply them in different ways. Lawande's aim was to create a new design capability within Harman, not to destroy or outsource it. As a result Harman is now in a stronger position because it can both produce the high-end systems still demanded by the luxury brands but it can also meet the exploding demand for lower-end, less complex systems in the mid-market. Those systems created for the developing world add to its offering in the developed world for mid-range cars, presented to squeezed middle-class consumers.

More developed world organisations will have to attempt this trick, so it is worth dwelling on some of what Harman did to pull it off. It set a binding constraint and a stretching goal which also created a sense of urgency: a product that would sell for half the price and be a third of the cost of traditional systems. This gave the team no option but to throw out the rulebook and work fast in new ways, in collaborative teams, with rapid development cycles, using standardised components and open source software. Yet perhaps the most important implication is that the most significant innovations of the new few years will not be at the cutting edge of technology but where familiar, low-cost technologies are applied in more inventive ways. The most important forms of innovation will be all about the application of known technologies to meet huge needs. The innovators who create these solutions will be the ones who recognise that need most clearly and urgently. Those innovators are likely to be close to the need while also having access to the technologies required. In the developed world our biggest disadvantage in reaching these solutions will be through being unable to let go and frightened to challenge conventional thinking about how our higher-spec, higher-cost systems need to work. We will need to make a special effort to think afresh.

Companies such as Harman are at the forefront of that effort. Many others – General Electric, Unilever, Procter & Gamble, Nokia and Samsung among them – are developing much more globally connected networks for innovation, to cross-pollinate ideas from the developing and the developed world. Out of this a new generation of products will emerge designed for low incomes – the consumers in the developing world – but applicable in time to consumers in the developed world on modest incomes, looking for a more effective, lower-priced solution to their needs. Yet we will need more than new products and services, we will need new systems, for health, education, transport and welfare. Creating those frugal systems which will be both lower-cost and more effective will involve alliances between public and private sectors. The ingredients for these new systems are now falling into place. A good example is how it is becoming possible to re-imagine health systems.

The Health Systems of the Future

The modern healthcare industry is arguably one of civilisation's greatest achievements: the organisation of knowledge, science, technology, people and care, on a vast scale to help fellow citizens live longer, healthier lives. It is also in deep trouble and for the foreseeable future it will become the site for the most significant, protracted innovation conflict in the developed world as reformers, managers, doctors and patients battle to change it.

Partly thanks to the success of modern public health programmes, people are living longer lives. At the beginning of the 20th century it was rare for someone to live much beyond the age of 70, and many died in childhood. Now the fastest-growing groups of the population in many developed countries are those over 65 and especially those over 80. This is a triumph. But it comes with a cost. People live longer lives but especially towards the end of those lives they are likely to have multiple chronic conditions, including perhaps forms of dementia, as well as arthritis, heart and lung conditions and diabetes. Ageing is placing huge burdens upon systems of care. The modern hospital-based system of healthcare was designed in response to the 19th-century toll of deaths from often short-lived but very intense infectious diseases which were the biggest killers at the turn of the 20th century. Now our biggest challenges come from multiple, often overlapping chronic conditions which people can live with for 20 years and more.

As medical science has become more specialised, so doctors are in a position to offer a wider array of diagnoses and treatments to patients who expect the best possible treatment almost regardless of the cost. As a result people with multiple chronic conditions can see several specialists, each with more sophisticated but also more costly treatments than their counterparts of 20 and 30 years ago. The result of this powerful inbuilt dynamic towards greater specialisation and so complexity, is rising costs. Our health systems are overengineered products of innovations driven primarily by doctors and pharmaceutical companies.

As a consequence, one of the main aims of health policy has become cost containment, alongside improving quality (which remains bewilderingly variable even within the same discipline) and improving access for those who are left in line queueing to see a doctor. That is why health systems in the developed world will be subject to repeated controversial reform programmes. Healthcare providers, regulators, funders and clients in the developed world are all searching for new models of care which deliver better outcomes – without costing more – by innovating approaches that blend technology, treatment, service and professional know-how in new ways. The health systems of the future, in the developed world, will focus more on the prevention and management of long-term conditions, working with people in their homes and communities, rather than taking them into expensive hospitals to be treated by doctors. Hospitals will still matter, especially for emergencies, acute cases and specialist expertise, but they will be surrounded by much more extensive, community-based networks of care, so people can be treated close to home, often by mobile, community health workers, equipped with smarter technologies. Many of the ingredients for these more preventative, community-based solutions are at hand. They come from innovations in the developing world being reverse engineered to work in the developed world. In the next decade we need to start importing those models into the developed world through a massive, concerted effort at reverse innovation, across every aspect of the health system.

These new systems will involve at least the following ingredients. They will use mobile technologies to aid diagnosis: a good example is Netra, a low-cost eye test developed by MIT Media Lab. Netra, which means 'eye' in Sanskrit, is a clip-on eye piece that can be attached to the top of a mobile phone and connected to the phone's LCD display. Looking into the eye piece, the user has to use the keys on their phone to align a series of dots until they all appear to overlap each other. This process is captured by an app in the phone which then calculates the extent to which the person's retina is out of alignment. That calculation provides a prescription for glasses.

The Netra equipment, which costs as little as $2, is a brilliant example of frugal innovation using digital technology. No trained professional is needed, nor a visit to an eye clinic: the phone's owner becomes an amateur optician. Whereas tradtional diagnostic kits are heavy and cumbersome, the Netra is portable and robust, and because it clips on and off it can be used on multiple phones. This is just one outstanding example among many of low-cost diagnostics.

As we saw earlier, MedicallHome in Mexico is providing the skeleton for a bare-bones primary healthcare system by connecting patients, doctors and providers through the mobile network. In the UK the NHS spent billions on an overengineered solution to this problem – called Connecting for Health – which has never worked. Borrowing from frugal approaches might be more effective. Medic Mobile started with humble beginnings in rural Malawi in the summer of 2007, with community health workers like Dickson Mtanga, a subsistence farmer, whose job it was to periodically walk 35 miles to gather and submit handwritten reports on 25 HIV+ patients in his community. Those reports were then sent by post to the main hospital in the region, which served 250,000 people in a 100-mile radius. The hospital relied on people like Dickson to be its front line. The system was costly, time-consuming and ineffective: there was no way to alert the hospital to arrange timely treatment. By using SMS technology and electronic records, health workers are now able to communicate, coordinate patient care and provide diagnoses. By using simple mobile technology Medic Mobile is able to bridge huge gaps in healthcare delivery in the developing world; treating patients more effectively and enabling the health provider to extend services to people who would otherwise not have received care. Frugal solutions like Medic Mobile probably have something to tell us about what could be achieved within our health systems. A related project, Mobile Academy in Bihar, is showing that thousands of community health workers, in the field, can be trained using modules downloaded by mobile phone. In the first year of the programme, launched in May 2012, more than 27,000 community health workers signed up for the course, and 8,000 have completed all the modules, at a minimal cost of just over Rs 100.

These innovations show it should be possible to support at much greater scale the kind of community-based, networked healthcare pioneered by the likes of Mothers-2-Mothers in Africa, the Neighbourhood Network for Palliative Care in Kerala and the inspirational Partners in Health working in Haiti and Peru. Each of these mobilises members of the local community, working alongside professionals, to provide daily, basic care and support for people, in or close to their homes. An early, leading example of how these innovations from the developing world could be reverse engineered into the developed world is the way the Partners in Health model has been adopted by its sister organisation, Prevention and Access to Care and Treatment (PACT) in Boston, to support people with HIV.

Partners in Health provides people with an *accompagnateur* – an accompanist – drawn from the local community to support them, not just in their interactions with the medical system, but as they cope at home with cooking and shopping, looking after their family and earning some money. Partners in Health found that with the right kind of accompanist they could successfully treat someone with TB, in their home, for about $200 compared with close on $15,000 in the US, where the person would be sent to hospital. PACT, created by Louise Behforouz, who worked on Partners in Health, does much the same for people in Boston on Medicaid suffering from HIV and long-term chronic conditions. Many schemes give community health workers walk-on parts as adjuncts to doctors who take centre stage; PACT puts community health workers at the centre of care, managing and calling in medical interventions when they are needed.

That is not all. Health systems will increasingly need to mobilise patients to help one another, as well. To be frugal they will have to become increasingly social. A pioneering example of what is possible here is Patients Like Me, an online network of more than 200,000 members, sharing their experiences of more than 2,000 medical conditions, providing mutual support, advice and a unique resource for researchers. Patients Like Me was started by the family of Stephen Heywood, who was diagnosed with ALS (also known as Motor Neurone Disease) at the age of just 29. Stephen was 37 when he died. In those eight years, he and his family searched for any new treatments, often operating on an agonisingly slow trial-and-error basis. Ben and James, Stephen's brothers, founded Patients Like Me in 2005, a little more than a year before he died. They began with the aim of connecting patients and their families to share their experiences of ALS: symptoms, treatments, relationships, sources of support. The community quickly flourished, their team grew, and communities for a whole range of other life-changing conditions were added: by 2009, they had 45,000 active members. By late 2013 the site had 200,000-plus members, with references to over 2,000 conditions: the original ALS network, now with 4,500 members, is the largest of its kind in the world. Crucially, the 200-strong Patients Like Me team has created a scientific approach, not just a social network. Members are encouraged to share data (treatment history, side-effects, hospitalisations, symptoms, disease-specific functional scores, weight, mood, quality of life) in standard ways: this data is then aggregated and presented back to them in a variety of ways. This both helps them to easily compare their experiences with the whole cohort who share their condition, and provides a rich and growing resource for use by medical researchers. Their in-house research team has published more than a dozen peer-reviewed papers and the site has been cited in more than 1,000 published scientific articles.

The core to all these approaches is that they see community assets, skills and relationships as key to both long-term health and effective, low-cost solutions. As a result they are less reliant on expensive, dedicated professionals, technologies and infrastructure. They piggyback on existing infrastructures, often providing services at home and in community centres. They use lay and para-professionals to provide services, calling in medical professionals only when needed. By shifting tasks out of hospitals and to para-professionals and peers in communities, these innovations leverage scarce professional knowledge over a far larger population. In the developed world these communitarian approaches could modernise and transform public health, mobilising social networks to promote behaviour change and enhance people's capacity to self-manage long-term conditions.

Alongside these stronger community networks for healthcare and prevention, there will be different kinds of hospitals. Some, like India's lean innovators – Lifespring in maternal health, Aravind in cataract operations and NH in heart operations – will do just one thing very well. Lean and specialised, these hospitals will provide a high-quality, high-volume, relatively low-cost service. Other innovators will go in the opposite direction, to extend and broaden their remit, to create integrated, seamless pathways to support people to live more healthily, rather than just treating their conditions efficiently when they become ill. Perhaps the leader in this regard is Valencia in southern Spain which has a system of payment for health outcomes which incentivises providers to find the most effective, low-cost method of healthcare provision, which often means helping people at home. The aim is to treat people and their conditions effectively, including improved prevention, rather than getting them into hospital.

These efforts all head in the same direction: towards greater integration of hospital and community, greater collaboration between doctor and patient, and more provision of technology, advice and support for people at home, from community-based health workers and peers. The key ingredients of the health systems of the future are being created in the developing world. The most potent way to reform our own overengineered and high-cost health systems is to import, absorb and adapt these models in the developed world. Those frugal systems of the future will: provide health in a different place, in the community rather than in institutions; see their purpose in a different way, focusing not just on medical conditions and disease but on health as prediction, prevention and living well; engage a wider range of people in care, including community health workers, peers and family members; make collaboration central to healthcare rather than just the provision of a professional service; adopt different models of finance and payment. The systems that adopt these frugal approaches to healthcare, especially for long-term conditions, will be the ones that can also afford the high-tech solutions that special cases need.

Frugal Freiburg

Cities will be one of the main sites for frugal innovation in the developed world, as civic innovators create new places to live which are affordable and economically successful because they are convivial and environmentally sustainable. Perhaps the finest current example of a frugal city is Freiburg in Germany, which has spawned a string of easy-to-use, overlapping innovations in housing, energy and transport that together make the city both highly social and clean.

Freiburg has undergone an unassuming and almost stealthy transformation in the past three decades. Whereas other cities have brazenly rebranded themselves with buildings and bridges designed by superstar architects to attract attention, Freiburg has remade itself through rather dull and functional innovation: clever forms of low-cost, self-build home ownership; combined heat and power schemes and the remaking of its humble tram system. The result is a city which is one of the greenest in Europe, family-friendly and affordable, a place where the squeezed middle class can live well despite their constrained incomes. As a result it is, like Curitiba, economically, socially and environmentally successful.

At the core of this combination is Freiburg's innovative approach to building low-cost housing for people on modest incomes. When the financial crisis led to the withdrawal of federal housing subsidies, Freiburg had no option but to seek alternative models. They started in a margin. The city adopted a form of shared, low-cost housing which had first been tried out in a nearby village on a very small scale.[84] The city acquired brownfield sites of land, a former barracks and a large industrial site, and equipped them with transport links and utilities. Residents were then invited to form *baugruppen* – groups which would get together to work with architects to build small blocks of flats. By clubbing together the residents got homes that cost 25 per cent below the market price. The city recouped its investments by selling land to the residents. Local builders and architects were employed. The low-rise developments were designed to be family-friendly, so that parents could call from a top-floor flat to children in the pedestrianised play areas below. In the most famous area of redevelopment, Vauban, scores of blocks were developed by different groups. All had to conform to some basic design rules, but they all had their own distinctive character. Riesfeld, the other main site for redevelopment, became a laboratory for hundreds of experiments with solar-powered homes.

Not only were the shared *baugruppen* homes more affordable to build, they were also designed to be cheap to live in. One key was to make them extremely energy efficient. The newer homes have extremely high-quality insulation to minimise heat wastage. About 25,000 houses in the city are heated entirely through a thermal waste treatment plant. (There may not be a long-term future in this form of energy: waste disposal has been cut sixfold in the last two decades. The average Freiburg resident generates just 114kg a year.) Much of the rest of the city is heated by 15 medium- to large-scale district heating plants which are like German versions of the Husk Power System of India. In Freiburg that idea has been taken to industrial scale across an entire city: half the city is heated that way. (Freiburg still has a long way to go to match Flensburg, a German town on the border with Denmark where 98 per cent of homes are supplied by a combined heat and power plant which will use 100 per cent renewable sources by 2050.) Where Freiburg flats have been refurbished with better standards of insulation, energy costs have been cut by 85 per cent, the kind of improvements in performance associated with frugal innovation in the developing world. In one pioneering block with the highest standards of insulation, built by a group of young families, a family living in a 90m² apartment pays just €90 a year for their energy compared with a German average household bill of close to €2,400. The basic costs of living in Freiburg will likely decline further as its ambitious plans for solar power kick in. Already home to half the domestic solar installations in Germany, Freiburg plans for more than 40 per cent of its energy to come from local, renewable sources in the near future.

The city's planners, however, were also determined to make the city easy to navigate and highly connected, as well as affordable. It is designed to be a city of short distances, so most amenities can be reached by walking. As other cities were getting rid of their old tram systems, Freiburg was extending its network to create a seamless system of trams, buses and light rail. In the past three decades car trips have declined, cycling has risen threefold and public transport journeys by a factor of two. Just over two-thirds of all trips in Freiburg are made by people walking, cycling or on public transport: many car-dependent US cities only manage a tenth of that. As the Freiburg public transport system is so well used it requires no subsidy: it pays for itself.

Freiburg, in short, is a thriving city because it has pursued a form of civic frugal innovation: minimising waste; investing in clean, shared social solutions; creating simple ways for people to build shared homes and use shared transport; promoting an easy conviviality and family-friendly atmosphere; reusing older technologies, like trams, and places to live on brownfield sites. There is nothing hair shirt about frugal Freiburg: it is a city that is living well but well within its means. The new ways of living we will all need in future will come from places like Freiburg.

Cities such as Freiburg, Curitiba, Copenhagen, Malmö and Portland show that we need not just frugal products and services but frugal systems for energy, housing, heating and transport to make life affordable and enjoyable. Those systems will require both new infrastructures and new patterns of behaviour, so people use them in new ways. Creating this mix will invariably involve public, social and private innovation, as it has done in Freiburg. Some of the most important sources of frugal innovation in the developed world will not be companies working alone but cities working with energy suppliers, bus companies, housebuilders, architects and others to create places to live which are lean and simple, shared and social, clean and sustainable.

Yet other kinds of frugal innovation will come from a completely different source: the reinvention of a craft tradition of making things locally.

Making it Together

The Raspberry Pi is a super simple, low-cost, credit card-sized computer, which is designed to make things. The machine is the brainchild of a group of computer scientists at Cambridge University who were alarmed by both the decline in the numbers of students applying to read Computer Science and the skills they lacked. Whereas in the 1990s most of the young people applying were coming for interview as experienced hobbyist programmers, having used basic machines such as the BBC Micro, Spectrum ZX and Commodore 64, the landscape in the 2000s was very different; a typical applicant might only have done a little web design. They would have grown up with more powerful, sophisticated computers and yet ironically would have been less capable of reprogramming and tinkering with them.

As computing became more ubiquitous, powerful, commercialised and consumer friendly, so the opportunity for young people to write their own computer programs all but evaporated. As the technology had become more sophisticated so it had also become less open to hobbyists and tinkerers. The Cambridge group decided part of the solution was to create a latter-day version of one of the basic machines on which they themselves first learned to program. They decided to innovate by retracing their steps to make a primitive, low-cost computer.

After about five years of tinkering, the group came up with a design for a basic, reprogrammable computer which in 2013 cost just £25, which is based on a chip designed for mobile phones, runs on open source software and is made under licence by a range of electronics manufacturers around the world. The Raspberry Pi Foundation, which they set up to make the computer, encourages other companies to clone its machine so it gets to as wide a market as possible.

Since its launch in 2012, more than 1.2 million Raspberry Pis have been sold to schools and students, but also to hobbyists making robots and parents with disabled children wanting to make their own monitoring devices, as well as museums and hospitals. Raspberry Pi is many innovations in one. Not only is it opening up basic programming to new generations, but it is also providing an ultra low-cost computer in the developing world. The Raspberry Pi is proof that often the best ideas come from looking backwards, to recuperate and reinvent approaches that have been discarded, and by looking sideways, to adapt innovations from other related industries – in this case using low-cost chips for mobile devices to make a computer.

The team, led by Eben Upton, had set out with few core design principles. Their computer would have to be appealing to children, so it would have to be able to play games and do useful things; it could not just be about programming. It had to be robust enough to recover from being dropped or stepped upon. To be programmable it had to come with embedded tools that would be easy to use. Most importantly, to be genuinely accessible for all it would have to be ultra cheap. They pegged the price at what they imagined an average school textbook would cost: £25. Upton describes it as a fantastic stretch goal, a binding constraint. They thought the market would be about 10,000 avid young programmers in the UK. Instead more than 200,000 Raspberry Pis were sold on the first day, to customers all over the world.

They managed to create a product with such powerful pull at such low cost by following frugal principles. Not only does it reuse chips designed for mobile phones, it also piggybacks on existing systems and resources. The Raspberry Pi avoids having a costly display by plugging into a television or a computer monitor. It will work with any keyboard and mouse. Sharing is also critical to the Raspberry Pi: everything runs on a version of the free and open source software Linux. Raspberry Pi, the £25 computer made in Cambridge, is a perfect example of genuinely radical, frugal innovation which could bring computing to those on very low incomes, as well as providing a digital Meccano set for aspiring young geeks in the developed world. Upton's team has achieved this by deploying the principles of frugal innovation: keep it lean and simple, reuse and share.

The Raspberry Pi is one part of a much larger movement, a civic surge of people making things, often in small batches, by using shared, open source designs downloaded from the web and simple, flexible, reprogrammable machines which draw on locally available resources. For its advocates, such as *Wired* editor Chris Anderson, this do-it-together makers' movement represents an opportunity to free ourselves from the tyranny of large, impersonal corporations making standardised, homogeneous products. But also it could be a route to a more frugal, self-sufficient economy, based on lower transport, energy and resource costs.[85] Anderson argues we are witnessing the emergence of a manufacturing economy which reflects both distributed and networked architecture of the web and its collaborative and entrepreneurial culture. This could create a new hybrid industrial economy, one which is simultaneously old and new as it combines the grass-roots ethic of Gandhian innovation with the scale and reach of the web and the power of modern digital technologies. In the West the makers' movement builds on a long, sometimes neglected tradition of hobbyist and craft producers, often working in sheds and garages, and the Pro-Am movement of consumer-innovators which is most famous for creating a string of extreme sports from windsurfing and mountain biking, to snowboarding and kitesurfing.

The components of this alternative industrial system include: cheap reprogrammable hardware such as the Arduino, a multi-purpose motherboard which like the Raspberry Pi can be put to many uses; low-cost 3D printers and fabrication labs which can make a wide range of basic products; open source libraries of designs, such as Thingiverse, for objects from bowls to shoes and bikes; festivals which bring together makers to show and share ideas, such as the hugely popular Maker Faire in the US; markets to sell home-made products such as the craft site Etsy, which now has 40 million customers and turns over $65 million a month; sites such as Threadless, Alibaba and MFG.com which allow people to place orders for custom-made manufactured products; alternative payment systems such as Square, designed to be used by smaller, collaborative producers; crowdfunding platforms such as Kickstarter, which allow these alternative producers to raise money to make their products a reality. It's not much of a step to imagine a more sophisticated version of the Echale a tu Casa brick-making machine being linked to the web to allow small communities to make a wide range of basic goods at low cost with little energy.

Anderson is a reporter: he is describing what is emerging in the world as it is. Eric Drexler is a visionary engineer who believes he can see how the world could become. His vision of a future in which we make things locally, for one another, is even more radical.

Drexler believes modern manufacturing, even in its latest lean incarnations, is still prodigiously wasteful and inefficient compared with biological systems which use local resources, renewable energy and leave behind little waste. Drexler, who made his reputation as a seer in the 1980s by bringing nanotechnology to popular attention, believes we are on the verge of a new industrial revolution, which he calls atomically precise manufacturing (APM). This would take the nascent decentralised maker movement to an entirely new level of scale and productivity.[86]

The best way to understand atomically precise manufacturing is to think of it as a bit like printing. A modern printer can translate a digital image from a computer into a series of pixels and then printed dots which create a physical replica of the digital original. Now imagine you could print off virtually any object you needed by first downloading a design and a recipe, and then minutely rearranging commonly available materials – carbon, hydrogen, oxygen, nitrogen – to make any material you needed. Atomically precise manufacturing would depend on our being able to reorganise materials from the inside out, almost reprogramming their molecular bonds, to create a variety of new materials from a few basic building blocks. Basic protein molecules are made up of 20 different kinds of monomers, strands which form their most basic components. The same basic monomers mixed in different ways can be found in soft rubber and hard plastics, in super strong spider silk and rhino horn. Imagine we were as clever as the mussel that can make its own hard shell without intense heat and attach itself securely to a rock while under water. If our manufacturing systems were that clever we could make a huge variety of objects out of the same basic set of materials without needing to forge, blast, sear or melt them. We stand, Drexler argues, on the verge of a frugal abundance: we could make virtually anything we want, out of common materials found locally, at very low cost, using renewable energy and leaving little waste. Lengthy, costly, energy-intensive supply chains would be a thing of the past. Old products could be broken down and reconverted back into the basic chemical feedstock needed to make new products. Instead of mines in ecologically sensitive parts of the world from which we take cobalt, tin and lead, we could instead rearrange widely available ingredients such as carbon, hydrogen and nitrogen. This would be a manufacturing system modelled on biological and chemical principles. We could have anything we want and yet still live lightly.

Drexler imagines a world in which each locality would have atomically precise manufacturing plants that would be fast, inexpensive and flexible, using digital designs, to churn out basic products at low cost, just as computers and mobile phones have made information and communications cheap and ubiquitous. Rather than producing electronic signals, APM systems would produce an endless array of physical products. Imagine a solar array being printed like a sheet of aluminium foil, or material as strong as steel being produced but without the blast furnace and the rolling mill. If APM machines were as widely spread as say mobile phone shops, product designs were available, open source and basic feedstock materials abundant, then millions of people could be lifted out of material poverty at low cost, using environmentally sustainable processes. It would be an ample sufficiency on a vast scale.

A Sign of Things about to Come

One sign of the extent of the demand for low-cost machines of the kind Drexler has in mind is the response to the super low-cost Aakash tablet computer. The Aakash was designed to cost about a week's salary for someone on a modest income, $5–10 a day, in the developing world: about $35. For most people in the developed world the Apple iPad is regarded as a second device, after their PC. The Aakash was intended to be the first and main computer for aspirational poorer consumers. Designed by Datawind, a Canada-based, UK-backed, Indian-inspired company, the Aakash was designed to be good enough, which means as good as the original iPad which was, lest we forget, regarded as revolutionary when it was launched. Datawind's aim is to equip millions of poorer families with a machine as good as the original iPad for a price of $35. It would be loaded with open source software and, by buying airtime wholesale on behalf of its consumers, Datawind is able to offer very low-cost, mobile Internet access.

The launch of the Aakash in India in 2011 triggered an avalanche of demand. Datawind's website was overwhelmed with what looked like a denial of service attack. Sackloads of cheques arrived in the post. The small call centre the company set up was deluged with more than 40,000 calls a day. The initial excitement quickly gave way to a sense of disappointment. Not everything went to plan. When the Indian government announced in 2011 a deal to buy the Aakash in bulk, it was in reality no more than a design idea. When Datawind started to make the Aakash it ran into enormous problems: the screen would freeze, the casing broke, the chip would pack in. The product went through at least three design iterations to eradicate the bugs.

Time and again radical and innovative products can fail and yet still open up a new market. Napster, the music file sharing system, may have closed, but not before it fatally exposed the vulnerability of the traditional music recording industry in the era of digital downloads and file sharing. Nothing would be quite the same again. The Aakash may yet be just such a revolutionary, disruptive failure. The excitement it has generated points to just how big a market there is for small, portable, robust and useful machines, which can be used by people living in poverty to improve their lives. Datawind took 4 million pre-orders. There are about 250,000 Apple iPads in India and just 30 million broadband connections in a country of more than 1 billion people. There are more than 900 million mobile phones. The market in India for ultra low-cost, simple, connected devices which can be tools of micro-productivity for people on modest incomes is vast: in India alone that market is 950 million people. The Aakash was the audacious idea that opened up that market, even if others following in its wake actually captured the opportunity. If someone comes along soon with a machine to make Drexler's atomically precise manufacturing possible, do not bet against people wanting it, in large numbers.

Datawind, the company that makes the Aakash, is not everyone's cup of tea. Critical reports in newspapers have queried its finances, the skills of its management and the quality of its products.[87] Yet Datawind too is a sign of what is to come: a small, cosmopolitan organisation, which brings together finance from the UK, know-how from Canada and engineers from India. Within two years of its launch as an idea in India, the Aakash was due to be on sale, as a real product, in the UK, for just under £40. That is how much time it took for an idea to become a product, take root in a developing world market and then flow back into the developed world's markets from whence it came. Frugal innovation is fed by cosmopolitan networks that channel ideas between the developed and developing world. What we are witnessing now with the mobile phone, the Raspberry Pi and the low-cost Aakash we might expect to happen to 3D printing and in time a version of Drexler's atomically precise manufacturing system inspired by a combination of biology and chemistry.

* * *

The centre of gravity for innovation is shifting. In the developed world the vast, squeezed middle classes are searching for ways to live well with less, in the context of restrained economic growth, resource constraints and climate change. Learning how to live well, but within our means, will be essential for households, companies and governments. That will lead people to husband their resources more carefully and spend more attentively, therefore choosing more carefully. We are in the market for frugal solutions, which will allow us to do much more with much less in some areas of our lives, so we can spend more on those things that really matter to us.

As that shift takes place so it will feed another: we will become more open to ideas, technologies and solutions which will flow back to the developed world from the poorer markets of the developing world. We will be in the market for solutions which often first proved themselves in the developing world. Ideas and technologies will flow in both directions. Technologies developed in the labs and university research departments of the rich world might find their first applications in the developing world and when they have become more established there they will find their way back to the lower end of richer markets in the developed world. A new global dynamic is taking shape in which ideas, applications and people flow in both directions. The diasporas and networked organisation that carry these flows will be the critical players in global innovation.

A new global dynamic is taking shape in which ideas, applications and people flow in both directions

These frugal solutions will take many routes into the lifestyles of consumers in the developed world. Some will be carried by large companies and lean producers, like Renault-Nissan, the leading pioneer of electric mobility; Unilever, which is attempting to increase its market share while cutting its carbon footprint by two-thirds, and General Electric, which has one of the most sophisticated global research and development networks. Another route might be through civic surge of the do-it-together makers' movement, a long tail of small-scale producers, enabled by the spread of open source designs and cheap reprogrammable machines for making basic objects. The digital technologies of the web, social media, big data and the Internet may yet find their real calling when they are harnessed to the job of creating real world products and more efficient systems for energy and transport, including through the social innovations of open source design, collaborative consumption and crowdfunding.

Yet frugal innovation will not succeed in the developed world unless it leads to new systems, not just new products and services. We need a new generation of lower-cost systems for energy and transport, health and education, which are more localised, decentralised and yet sustainable and efficient. Those systems will draw on the design lessons of natural systems, which use local resources, renewable energy and leave little waste. The transition from the high-energy, high-cost, wasteful industrial systems we have to these newer, more sustainable and flexible systems, will require innovation at many levels, from new niches where new products – like electric cars – will be piloted to new infrastructures (battery recharging stations) and the public policies to promote them. In other words it will be a protracted struggle as we wrestle with older, outdated systems which are well dug-in, familiar and operate at vast scale. In many of these fields innovation will be exciting but also bring with it unsettling conflict as new systems jostle to displace old. Perhaps our greatest hope should be in frugal cities, places like Freiburg, which are lean, clean and social, where new systems enable people on modest incomes to enjoy a high-quality and sustainable way of life.

12

Our Frugal Future

We find ourselves in an uncomfortable, confusing position, seemingly trapped between utopia and oblivion.[88]

On the one hand, we have the prospect held out by techno-utopian optimists such as Eric Drexler and others of a radical abundance brought to us by machines that will allow us to make whatever we want at low cost, locally and without making undue calls on natural resources. On the other, we have pessimists such as Stephen Emmott, who fear innovation is feeding our appetites for more products, which use more resources and will speed us toward a future of environmental catastrophe and a war of all against all for control of scarce resources. The most perplexing aspect of living in an economy driven by accelerating technological innovation is that although we create technology we do not necessarily understand what it is for, let alone control it. Frugal innovation provides an alternative to this choice between bleak pessimism and fantastical optimism and a hope that we might be able to control how we use technology to put it to good use. That is because frugal innovation provides us with both a purpose and ethic to guide innovation and a method to make it happen. That combination should allow us to make better choices, together, about how we make the future.

Ask for What is Impossible

Frugal innovators start by asking questions that risk making them sound stupid. The questions sound preposterous because they invite solutions which seem impossible within the confines of conventional thinking. One of the advantages of frugal innovators is that they often deliberately put themselves in extreme conditions where they have no alternative but to ask such questions.

Charlie Paton asked whether it would be possible to make water from thin air using nothing more than the power of the sun. Ralph Bistany is asking whether it is possible to create a school where children teach themselves. Suresh Kumar asked for a health system in which most of the work is not done by doctors, in hospitals, but by friends and neighbours in homes. Gyanesh Pandey asked why it would not be possible for the poorest people to get electricity from waste they threw away every day. Madhav Chavan demanded to know how to educate a child to ready them for school for just $10 a year. The water engineers of Singapore wondered what it would take for a city to become its own reservoir and the organic farmers of Havana had no option but to ask how a city could feed itself.

So if your company, school, hospital, organisation wants to get started on frugal innovation get used to asking questions the answers to which sound impossible, outlandish and far-fetched. You have to court the possibility that you will sound slightly mad.

Thrive on Crisis, Work in Margins

Many frugal innovators started in the midst of a crisis which threatened their very survival. Existential crisis, a threat to their existence, provoked a radical response. Sabis leapt forward due to the Lebanese civil war; Toyota created lean production because it was on the verge of going out of business; Singapore devised its water recycling system because the alternative was severe drought and rationing; Havana started growing its own food after the collapse of its export markets for sugar in the Soviet Union. That, however, is just the starting point. Crisis breeds a sense of urgency and common purpose. Conventional wisdom, the approaches that work in normal conditions, has to be discarded. In crisis people start to cooperate, improvise and pitch in.

Crisis breeds a sense of urgency and common purpose

Frugal innovators often start in marginal, niche markets, overlooked by large companies and government departments. They thrive on their marginality; they do not need to be associated with respectable insiders with lots of resources. They see that being on the margins gives them a vantage point which allows them to turn the world upside down. So if you want to follow the path of frugal innovation start in places where doing what seems mad by the rules of conventional wisdom makes perfect sense. Frugal innovators use their weaknesses, their marginal position and lack of resources to work in their favour. They thrive on asymmetry: radical change comes from marginal markets; those without resources have no option but to be radical innovators; constraints breed creativity.

Welcome constraints

Frugal innovators welcome extreme constraints – lack of resources and consumers who cannot afford expensive products – as a spur to radical innovation. Frugal innovators make these constraints work to their advantage, breaking through conventional wisdom to find new designs, business models and product architectures. Frugal innovation is like ju-jitsu, a martial art in which the skill is to use your opponent's force and weight to throw them over. Often traditional innovation programmes start by freeing innovators from constraints, giving them time, money and places to re-imagine the future, free from inhibitions. That can work. But frugal innovators work in a completely different way. The imposition of tight, binding constraints drives their creativity.

Learn to be Lean

Get used to asking: can this be done in a leaner way, with fewer resources and without dedicated, fixed machines and equipment? Can you eliminate waste generated by bureaucracy by giving more power to the front line, including consumers, to deliver solutions? Lean processes locate decision making as close as possible to where value is created for the customer, on a shop floor, in a classroom, at a patient's bedside. The more bureaucracy there is, the longer it takes to get a decision and the more time and other resources get wasted. Lean innovation takes continual efforts to weed out every delay, diversion and form of waste, to find the most direct, efficient, smooth flow of people and processes. Lean is simultaneously more efficient and elegant because there is less friction in a lean system.

Simplify

Ask how your product can be simplified in the most elegant and effective way to focus resources on what generates the most value for consumers. This will mean really understanding what matters to consumers and focusing on those key features which deliver most of the value. How can a product be redesigned so that it eliminates the need for a detailed manual, specialist knowledge and special conditions in which to work? Simplicity is not just about taking out features from complex products. A new product can be made to feel simple if it seems familiar and therefore easy to use, like the oxytocin spray modelled on an aerosol. Products and services that provide a complete, end-to-end solution are simpler than standalone products that do not really work without ancillary services and software. A brick-maker is not much good unless you have a plan for what to do with the bricks and the money and people needed to build the houses. A fire engine is vital in a crisis, to put out a fire – a heavy-duty, complex, professional, sophisticated solution – but the best way to prevent deaths in fires is to stop the fires happening in the first place and the most effective way to do that is to fit smoke alarms in more houses. The smoke alarm is a simple, low-cost, distributed, preventative and frugal solution to the challenge of making sure people do not die in a fire. It helps prevent the fire. The fire engine is a costly, fixed and specialist service which is crucial in an emergency. We need more smoke alarm solutions.

To Create Value, Share it

Frugal innovators regard the social aspects of their business as core to the solutions they offer. Delivering a solution to people, especially one that involves lengthy supply chains and specialists, can be expensive. Equipping people to solve a problem themselves, with one another, is much more cost-effective. Frugal innovators derive profound advantages from cooperative forms of organisation: do-it-together. The pursuit of their social mission is a spur to be more efficient. Their ability to organise shared solutions allows them to make better use of scarce resources. By working closely with and often employing people from the communities that they serve, they get access to informal, tacit forms of knowledge that are highly valuable. Their ability to become social movements can mobilise additional resources. Their reliance on peer-to-peer networks helps them to spread innovations through word of mouth. Frugal innovators create social, shared models of business not just because they believe in them but because they create a source of advantage: they are more efficient and effective as a result. Can the solution to the challenge you face be social, something that people create with themselves, do-it-together, rather than delivered to and for them each time they need it?

Waste is Fuel

Lean, low-cost solutions can be even more environmentally costly if they simply generate higher demand without cutting back on the resources used per capita and in absolute terms. Frugal solutions have to be lean, simple, low-cost *and* clean. Clean is not an add-on: it has to be central to the design of the solution. Frugal systems, especially for water and energy, have to be designed around natural cycles, to reuse, recycle, repurpose and remake as much as they can. Where innovation has been associated with the invention of the new, from scratch, using additional resources, it will instead have to involve 're'-thinking – allowing us to make better use of what we already have. That means we will need new technologies that will simultaneously go forwards and backwards, to reinvent old-fashioned rain harvesting, market gardens, local cisterns, ponds and gasification plants in the era of the sprawling urban metropolis. Natural design principles – use local resources, keep energy demand low, exploit diversity, recycle all waste – will be increasingly important in the future.

Blend, Do Not Invent

Frugal innovators are great blenders. They rarely invent entirely new solutions, using new technologies. They prefer to create new solutions using older, proven, tried-and-tested technologies, which are easy to maintain, simple to use and cheap to buy. They like nothing more than borrowing an already effective idea from somewhere else if it saves them having to invest in something from scratch. Solutions that reuse existing ideas and technologies, like gasification powered by discarded rice husks, are often simpler than leading-edge technologies and that means they require limited new learning.

Frugal innovators create solutions that blend basic ingredients in many different ways. Lean solutions tend to be clean because they eliminate waste in all forms. When products, services and systems are simpler it is easier for them to be lean and efficient. Simpler systems break down less and are easier to fix. Frugal innovations succeed by having a strong social component because they have to get close to their customers, to understand their lives and to seek out opportunities for the intelligent sharing of resources, which allows people to use just as much as they need. Shared solutions often generate lean outcomes: resources are used more intensively, with less waste and duplication. Most lean systems rely on communities of suppliers, workers and customers sharing information. Individualised ownership solutions are inflexible; they duplicate costly assets, many of which lie idle for long periods.

Frugal innovation is at its most effective and powerful when the four basic ingredients are blended together so that they feed one another in a self-reinforcing cycle: lean and simple, clean and social.

Think Like a Movement

Innovation is stillborn unless it brings about widespread changes to behaviour. A new system only comes to life when consumers start to use it en masse, changing their behaviour as they do so. Madhav Chavan has created a movement for better education in India. Suresh Kumar created a movement to support people at the end of their lives. Singapore made itself almost self-sufficient in water by creating a movement to conserve and use water more intelligently. Havana feeds itself because growing local vegetables became a movement. The *baugruppen* in Freibiurg are a movement. New products spread most effectively through word of mouth as consumers emulate and imitate one another, learning how to use something new from one another. If you want to bring about large-scale change, with few resources, then you have to think like a movement, to mobilise people to devote their own time, resources and skills for the sake of the movement. New markets, for novel approaches to clean energy, organic food, public health, are often opened up first by social movements, pressing for the adoption of a different ethic of consumption and production. Movements often make new markets. The frugal innovators of the future, for example those creating transport systems based on electric cars, will have to create a consumer movement around their product as well as an infrastructure to make using an electric car easier.

Innovate New Business Models

Frugal innovators are especially inventive in working out their business models: how they create value and share it with consumers, investors and employees. Business model innovation is an essential part of the toolkit. The NH heart hospitals have a hybrid model in which they charge some patients a full fee for a first-class service and then give other patients free operations. The sense of social mission embedded in this direct cross-subsidy helps to motivate the doctors. Often frugal innovators like Pratham and M2M are organisational innovators. They work like radicants, putting down roots as they spread, drawing on locally available resources through adaptive forms of franchising: the Chinese restaurant model of spread, rather than McDonald's. Many are devising different ways for consumers to save and to pay for their products: Echale a tu Casa is becoming a savings programme, so people living in near poverty in rural Mexico can save to build houses using the bricks it helps them make; Husk Power Systems and Saravjal, the water kiosks, are modelling their services on pre-paid mobile phones. Even if a product works and even if consumers like it, an organisation still has to find a sustainable way, and often that means a profitable way, to provide it. Working creatively with low-income, cash-strapped consumers means innovating in how they save and pay for what they use, not just in the product itself.

These ten rules of thumb should guide innovation in the 21st century. Frugal innovators are finding a way to pull off apparently astounding feats, by turning conventional wisdom on its head. If we follow these principles then we stand a chance of tackling the immense challenges we face. If we decide to turn our backs on them then we will continue to innovate but in a way that will only make our position worse.

Business will be the central player in this frugal wave but only if companies find a deeper sense of social purpose to guide how they make money. The best companies, the most successful brands, help us to learn how to live better, more fulfilled, successful lives. They make money as a by-product of their social purpose. The main role of business in society should be to help us learn: how to make better use of our energy resources; new ways to communicate; new ways to save for our retirement or life in old age. All of business, and especially all of business innovation, should be part of an attempt to help us to learn how to live better lives. The most creative, successful businesses of the future will enable us to learn to live more successfully, within the tightening constraints that we face. That is why our future will depend on frugal innovation to help us learn how to live well, while using fewer resources.

References

1. Jim O'Neill, *The Growth Map: Economic Opportunity in the BRICs and Beyond* (Portfolio Penguin, 2013).
2. Flamingo (various contributors), *Getting to Know Planet Earth's New Urban Majority* (Flamingo, London, 2011).
3. Santosh Desai, *Mother Pious Lady: Making Sense of Everyday India* (Harper Collins India, 2010).
4. Douglas Saunders, *Arrival City: How the Biggest Migration in History is Reshaping Our World* (Cornerstone, 2011).
5. Adam Lent and Mathew Lockwood, 'Creative Destruction: Putting Innovation at the Heart of Progressive Economic Policy', Institute of Public Policy Research, December 2010.
6. Lent and Lockwood, 'Creative Destruction'.
7. Avner Offer, *The Challenge of Affluence: Self-Control and Well Being in the United States and Britain Since 1950* (Oxford University Press, 2007).
8. 'The Lost Decade of the Middle Class', Pew Social Trends, August 2012.
9. The Resolution Foundation, *Squeezed Britain 2013*, Resolution Foundation, London 2013; Sophia Parker (ed.), *The Squeezed Middle: The Pressure on Ordinary Workers in America and Britain*, Resolution Foundation 2013.
10. Joshua Field Millburn and Ryan Nicodemus, *Simplicity: Essays* (Asymmetrical Press, 2012).
11. Courtney Carver, *Living in the Land of Enough* (Amazon, 2011).
12. Stephen Emmott, *Ten Billion* (Penguin, 2013).
13. John Robert McNeill, *Something New Under the Sun: An Environmental History of the Twentieth Century* (W. W. Norton, 2001).
14. McKinsey Global Institute, McKinsey Sustainability & Resource Productivity Practice, 'Resource Revolution: Meeting the World's Energy, Materials, Food, and Water Needs', McKinsey & Company, November 2011.

15. Peter A. Senge, Bryan Smith, Nina Kruschwitz, Joe Laur and Sara Schley, *The Necessary Revolution: How Individuals and Organizations are Working Together to Create a Sustainable World* (Nicholas Brealey, 2008).

16. Nicholas Stern, *The Stern Review on the Economics of Climate Change* (HM Treasury, 2006).

17. Bill McKibben, *Deep Economy: The Wealth of Communities and the Durable Future* (Times Books, 2007).

18. See http://www.footprintnetwork.org.

19. See http://www.unep.org/maweb/en/index.aspx.

20. McKinsey, 'Resource Revolution'.

21. Asit K. Biswas and Cecilia Tortajada, 'Water Supply of Phnom Penh: An Example of Good Governance', *International Journal of Water Resources Development*, 26:2 (2010), 157–72.

22. Mary Midgley, *Gaia: The Next Big Idea* (Demos, London, 2001).

23. Paul Collier, *The Plundered Planet: How to Reconcile Prosperity with Nature* (Penguin, 2011).

24. See, for example, The Circular Economy Report, The Ellen Macarthur Foundation, http://www.ellenmacarthurfoundation.org/business/reports.

25. Carol Dweck, *Mindset: How You Can Fulfil Your Potential* (Random House, 2006).

26. Navi Radjou, Jaideep Prabhu and Simone Ahuja, *Jugaad Innovation: Think Frugal, Be Flexible, Generate Breakthrough Growth* (Josey Bass, 2012); Kirsten Bound and Ian Thornton, 'Our Frugal Future: Lessons from India's Innovation System', Nesta, July 2012. Available from www.nesta.org.uk.

27. See: http://www.sristi.org/hbnew/.

28. Dan Breznitz and Michael Murphree, *Run of the Red Queen: Government, Innovation, Globalization and Economic Growth in China* (Yale University Press, 2011); Bound, Kirsten, Tom Saunders, James Wilsdon and Jonathon Adams, 'China's Absorptive State: Research, Innovation and the Prospects for China-UK Collaboration', Nesta, 2013. Available from www.nesta.org.uk.

29. Don Tapscott and Anthony Williams, *Wikinomics: How Mass Collaboration Changes Everything* (Atlantic Books, 2007).

30. E. F. Schumacher, *Small is Beautiful: Economics As If People Mattered* (Vintage, 1993).

31. Victor Papanek, *Design for the Real World, Human Ecology and Social Change* (Thames and Hudson, 1985).

32. Cynthia Smith, *Design for the Other 90%* (Cooper Hewitt Museum, 2008).

33. Paul Polak and Mal Warwick, *The Business Solution to Poverty: Designing Products and Services for Three Billion New Consumers* (Berrett-Koehler, 2013).

34. Hystra, 'Marketing Innovative Devices for the Bottom of the Pyramid', Hystra. com, 2013; Ted London, Stuart L. Hart and Eric Kacou, *Business Strategies for the Bottom of the Pyramid* (FT Collections, 2013).

35. C. K. Prahalad, *Fortune at the Bottom of the Pyramid* (Pearson Education India, 2009).

36. Ted London and Stuart L. Hart, *Next Generation Business Strategies for the Base of the Pyramid* (FT Press, 2011).

37. Paul Hawken, Amory Lovins and Hunter Lovins, *Natural Capitalism: Creating the Next Industrial Revolution* (Back Bay Books, 2000).

38. Paul Hawken, *The Ecology of Commerce: A Declaration of Sustainability* (Harper Paperbacks, revised edn, 2010).

39. Bound and Thornton, 'Our Frugal Future'.

40. James P. Womack, Daniel T. Jones and Daniel Roos, *The Machine that Changed the World – The Story of Lean Production* (Free Press, 1990); Jeffrey Liker, *The Toyota Way, 14 Management Principles from the World's Greatest Manufacturer* (McGraw-Hill, 2003).

41. James P. Womack and Daniel T. Jones, *Lean Thinking: Banish Waste and Create Wealth in Your Corporation* (Productivity Press, 2003).

42. James Tooley, *From Village School to Global Brand: Changing the World through Education* (Profile Books, 2012).

43. James Tooley, *The Beautiful Tree: A Personal Journey into how the World's Poor are Educating Themselves* (Cato Institute, 2009).

44. Geeta Gandhi Kingdon, 'The Progress of School Education in India', GPRG-WPS-071. Oxford and Swindon: Global Poverty Research Group and Economics and Social Research Council. See www.gprg.org.

45. Quoted in Tooley, *The Beautiful Tree*.

46. See http://www.echale.com.mx.

47. Donald A. Norman, *The Design of Everyday Things* (MIT Press UK, 1998).

48. John Maeda, *The Laws of Simplicity* (MIT Press, 2006).

49. Shalabh Kumar Singh, Ashish Gambhir, Alexi Sotiropoulus and Stephen Duckworth, 'Frugal Innovation: Learning from Social Entrepreneurs in India', Serco Institute, 2012.

50. Clayton Christensen, *The Innovator's Dilemma: When New Technologies Cause Great Firms to Fail* (Harvard Business School Publishing, 1997).

51. Donald Norman, *Living with Complexity* (MIT Press, 2010).

52. Ron Adner, *Wide Lens: A New Strategy for Innovation* (Portfolio Penguin, 2012).

53. Madhav Chavan, 'From Schooling to Learning', see http://www.pratham.org/.

54.

55. Esther Duflo and Abhijit Banerjee, *Poor Economics: A Radical Rethinking of the Way to Fight Global Poverty* (Public Affairs, 2011).

56. The Lancet Commission, 'Technologies for Global Health', *The Lancet*, 380 (4 August 2012) 507–35.

57. 'From Gap to Opportunity: Business Models for Scaling up Energy Access', International Finance Corporation, 2012.
58. See http://www.huskpowersystems.com/.
59. See Hystra, 'Marketing Innovative Devices'.
60. Janine M. Benyus, *Biomimicry: Innovation Inspired by Nature* (William Morrow & Co., 2002).
61. Hawken, Lovins and Lovins, *Natural Capitalism*.
62. Steven Solomon, *Water: The Epic Struggle for Wealth, Power and Civilisation* (Harper Collins, 2010).
63. Fred Pearce, *When the Rivers Run Dry: What Happens When Our Water Runs Out?* (Eden Project Books, 2007).
64. Quoted in Pearce, *When the Rivers Run Dry*.
65. Smith, *Design for the Other 90%*.
66. See http://en.wikipedia.org/wiki/LifeStraw.
67. Rajnish Tiwari and Cornelius Herstatt, 'Frugal Innovations for the Unserved Customer: An Assessment of India's Attractiveness as Lead Market for Cost-effective Products, Technology and Innovation Management', Hamburg University of Technology, Working Paper, March 2012.
68. Jonathan Margolis, 'Look What I Grew in the Desert', *The Observer Magazine*, 25 November 2012.
69. Pearce, *When the Rivers Run Dry*.
70. Polak and Warwick, *The Business Solution to Poverty*.
71. Hystra, 'Marketing Innovative Devices'.
72. One of the cities in the world with the most effective, well-managed public water systems is the Cambodian capital Phnom Penh. The city's water supply system has innovated in the crisis left behind by the disastrous Khmer Rouge regime, which killed millions and depopulated the city. By the 1990s the city's water system had just five engineers and had lost 70 per cent of its water. The pressure in the system was so low that many households connected to it could not get water. Using very basic techniques of better, lean management, water metering and billing, the Phnom Penh Water Services Authority since the late 1990s has increased water production by 437 per cent, extended the distribution network by 557 per cent and reduced water wastage to 6 per cent, far lower than most cities in the developed world. (Thames Water, the main water utility in London, loses about 25 per cent of the water in its system through leakage.) Biswas and Tortajada, 'Water Supply of Phnom Penh'.
73. Yong Soon Tan, *Clean, Green and Blue: Singapore's Journey towards Environmental and Water Sustainability* (Institute of South East Asian Studies, 2008).
74. Dan Cruickshank, *A Tale of Two Cities*, BBC2, 2012.

75. McKibben, *Deep Economy*.
76. Marc Levinson, *The Box: How the Shipping Container Made the World Smaller and the Economy Bigger* (Princeton University Press, 2006).
77. Eric Ries, *The Lean Startup: How Constant Innovation Creates Radically Successful Businesses* (Crown Publishing, 2011).
78. The story of Partners in Health, PACT and the accompaniment model is told in several places. One of them is Vijay Govindrajan and Chris Trimble, *Reverse Innovation: Create Far from Home, Win Everywhere* (Harvard Buisiness Review Press, 2012).
79. Tina Rosenberg, *Join the Club: How Peer Pressure Can Transform the World* (W. W. Norton, 2011); Alex Bentley, Mark Earls and Michael O'Brien, *I'll Have What She's Having: Mapping Social Behavior* (MIT Press 2011).
80. Charles Leadbeater, 'It's Cooperation, Stupid', Institute for Public Policy Research (IPPR), 2012.
81. Jimmy Greer, 'Brazilintel'. http://blogs.ft.com/beyond-brics/2013/04/17/guest-post-brazil-and-the-case-for-muddle-through-ology/#axzz2T9Ga0Rmc.
82. Annalee Saxenian, *The New Argonauts* (Harvard University Press 2007); Kathleen Newland (ed.), *Diasporas: New Partners in Global Development Policy* (Migration Policy Institute, 2010).
83. Govindrajan and Trimble, *Reverse Innovation*.
84. Peter Hall, *Good Cities, Better Lives* (Routledge, 2013).
85. Chris Anderson, *Makers: The New Industrial Revolution* (Random House Business Books, 2012).
86. Eric Drexler, *Radical Abundance: How a Revolution in Nanotechnology will Change Civilisation* (Public Affairs, 2013).
87. An early sceptical review of the Aakash came from http://www.nytimes.com/2012/12/30/technology/indias-aakash-venture-produces-optimism-but-few-computers.html.
88. Richard Buckminster Fuller, *Utopia or Oblivion: The Prospects for Humanity* (Viking, 1972).

Bibliography

Bhatti, Yasser and Marc Ventresca, 'The Emerging Market for Frugal Innovation, Fad, Fashion or Fit?'. Working Paper, Social Science Research Network. http://papers.ssrn.com/sol3/papers.cfm?abstract_id=2005983.

Biswas, Asit K. and Tortajada, Cecilia, 'Water Supply of Phnom Penh: An Example of Good Governance', *International Journal of Water Resources Development*, 26:2 (2010), 157–72.

Botsman, Rachel and Roo Rogers, *What's Mine is Yours: How Collaborative Consumption is Changing the Way We Live*, Collins, 2011.

Bound, Kirsten and Ian Thornton, 'Our Frugal Future: Lessons from India's Innovation System', Nesta, 16 July 2012. http://www.nesta.org.uk/publications/our-frugal-future-lessons-india%C2%92s-innovation-system.

Bound, Kirsten, Tom Saunders, James Wilsdon and Jonathon Adams, 'China's Absorptive State, Research, Innovation and the Prospects for China-UK Collaboration', Nesta, October 2013. http://www.nesta.org.uk/sites/default/files/chinas_absorptive_state_0.pdf.

Brand, Stewart, *Whole Earth Discipline: An Ecopragmatist Manifesto*, Viking Penguin, 2009.

Dobbs, Richard, Jeremy Oppenheim and Fraser Thompson, 'Mobilizing for a Resource Revolution', *McKinsey Quarterly*, 1 January (2012).

Freeland, Chrystia, 'Getting by without the Middle Class', *International Herald Tribune*, 10 June 2011.

Gansky, Lisa, *The Mesh: Why the Future of Business is Sharing*, Portfolio Penguin, 2010.

Haque, Umair, *The New Capitalist Manifesto: Building a Disruptively Better Business*, Harvard University Press, 2011.

Hawken, Paul, *The Ecology of Commerce: A Declaration of Sustainability*, Harper Business, 1993.

Hesseldahl, Peter, 'Progress in Learning and Innovation, Jugaad: The Indian Style of Innovation', Universe Foundation, Report, October 2012.

Hester, Randolph T., *Design for Ecological Democracy*, Massachusetts Institute of Technology Press, 2009.

Hystra, 'Marketing Innovative Devices for the Bottom of the Pyramid', Hystra. com, 2013. http://hystra.com/marketing-devices/.

Kuznetsov, Yevgeny, 'Diaspora Networks and the International Migration of Skills: How Countries Can Draw on Their Talent Abroad', World Bank Institute, WBI Development Studies, 15 November 2006.

McKibben, Bill, *Deep Economy: The Wealth of Communities and the Durable Future*, Times Books, 2007.

McKinsey & Company, 'Emerging Markets on the Move: How to Seize a $30 Trillion Opportunity', *McKinsey Quarterly*, 4 (2012).

McKinsey Global Institute, McKinsey Operations Practise, 'Manufacturing the Future: The Next Era of Global Growth and Innovation', McKinsey & Company, November 2012.

McKinsey Global Institute, McKinsey Sustainability & Resource Productivity Practice, 'Resource Revolution: Meeting the World's Energy, Materials, Food, and Water Needs', McKinsey & Company, November 2011.

Margolis, Jonathan, 'Look What I Grew in the Desert', *The Observer Magazine*, 25 November 2012.

Neate, Rupert, 'Recession Bypasses World of Luxury Goods', *The Guardian*, 16 February 2013.

Newland, Kathleen (ed.), *Diasporas: New Partners in Global Development Policy*, Migration Policy Institute, November 2010.

Norman, Donald A., *The Design of Everyday Things*, Massachusetts Institute of Technology Press, 1998.

Pew Research, 'The Lost Decade of the Middle Class'. http://www.pewsocial trends.org/2012/08/22/the-lost-decade-of-the-middle-class/.

Pilloton, Emily, *Design Revolution: 100 Products that are Changing People's Lives*, Thames & Hudson, 2009.

Rogers, Matt, 'Five Technologies to Watch', *McKinsey Quarterly*, 1 (2012).

Rosenberg, Tina, *Join the Club: How Peer Pressure can Transform the World*, W. W. Norton, 2011.

Schwarz, Michiel and Joost Elffers, *Sustainism is the New Modernism: A Cultural Manifesto for the Sustainist Era*, Distributed Arts, 2011.

Senge, Peter, Bryan Smith, Nina Kruschwitz, Joe Laur and Sara Schley, *The Necessary Revolution: How Individuals and Organizations are Working Together to Create a Sustainable World*, Nicholas Brealey, 2008.

Tilder, Lisa and Beth Blotstein (eds.), *Design Ecologies: Essays on the Nature of Design*, Princeton Architectural Press, 2008.

Index

A

Aakash   177–8
Acumen Fund   55, 146
Afghanistan   110
Africa   15, 16, 42, 52, 72, 73, 75, 92–4, 96, 105, 121–3, 152, 166
  Mutate   18
  schools   73
Ahuja, Simone   52
AIDS   122, 152
  see also HIV
Airbnb   130
Alaska   118
Alibaba   175
Altenfelder, Felipe   131–5
America   26, 122, 145, 159
  Americans   27
  American dream   26, 32, 131
  American goods   24
  Central America   1
  Latin America   16, 64
  see also US
Anderson, Chris   174–5
Apple   48
  iPhone   83
  iPod   83
  iPad   177–8
Aravind   168

Architecture for Humanity to
  Archeworks   55
Arduino   174
ASER review   89
Asia   1, 105
  East Asia   72
  South Asia   72, 92
Audi   11, 17, 160–1
Australia   1, 91, 109, 143
  Port Augusta   108
  Queensland   120
Australian National University   106

B

Babauta, Leo   30
Balsakhi programme   89
Balwadi   87–8
Banerji, Dr Rukmini   86
Bangalore   58–9, 61, 142
  Hosur Road   58, 60
Bangladesh   72, 96, 100
  Dhaka   4, 16
Barefoot Power   100
BBC Micro   172
Beatles   20
Behforouz, Louise   167
  see also PACT
Benetton   22
Bentley   12

Berkeley, University of California 131–3

Besser, Mitch 122–4, 135, 156

Bihar, India 166

Biocon 60

Bistany, Ralph 71, 74–5, 182

Blockbuster 31

Bloemink, Barbara 54

BMW 160

Boston 166–7

Brand, Stewart 132

Brazil 6, 10, 52, 76, 132, 148, 150

  Brazilians 11, 16, 72, 131, 133–4

  Creluz 99

  Cujaru 149

  Curitiba 147–8, 150

  Curitiba's Institute of Public Policy 150

  Instituto de Pesquisa Planejamento Urbano de Curitiba 150

  Parana 133, 150

BRICs 10–11, 18

Bridge International Academy Network 73

  see also Kenya,

Britain 17, 19, 145

  British 16, 108

  British government 38

Brown, Lester 38

Buenos Aires 16

C

California 2, 24, 50, 108

Cambodia 99

Cambridge University 172, 174

  Cambridge University Engineering Programme for Socially Responsible Design 54

Canada 27, 177–8

Cairo 16

Cape Town 122

Carver, Courtney 30

CERN 35

Chanel 12

Chavan, Madhav 86, 88–9, 147, 157, 182, 187

Chicago 55

  Chicago University 86

China 6, 10, 11–12, 16, 23–4, 38–9, 51, 53, 75, 119, 160, 162

  Gansu Province 110

  Shanghai 16, 142

Christenson, Clayton 48, 82

Chuagxin, Zizhu 52

climate change 6, 15, 35, 38, 97, 178

cloud computing 130

Coca-Cola 21

Colgate 22

Columbia 64, 76

  schools 76

College of Social Work 86–7

  see also Vasantik Varga

Collier, Paul 43

collateralised debt obligation (CDO) 24

Commodore 64 172

Copenhagen 51, 99, 172

Cornell University 55

  Johnson School of Management 55

Couchsurfing 130

Coursera 75

Crest 22

D

Datawind 177–8

Delhi, India 9, 16

Denmark 171

Detroit 65

DHL 125

Didi 87

Domino's 150

Dr Who 20

Drexler, Eric   175–7, 178, 181
    automatically precise manufacturing
        (APM)   175–6
Drupal   130
Duke University   93
Dweck, Carol   51

E
EasyJet   81
e-book   84–5
Echale e tu Casa   78–81, 84, 127, 143,
    155, 175, 188
Ecuador   64, 72
Edison, Thomas   155
education   2, 3, 6, 8, 15, 17–18, 20–1,
    32, 69, 71, 72–6, 86, 88–90, 127,
    145, 180, 182
Elffers, Joost   57
Emmott, Stephen   35, 181
energy   2, 4–6, 18, 27, 34–44, 56,
    79, 81, 91, 97–99, 101–8, 114,
    117, 120, 159, 169–72, 174–6,
    179–80, 186–8
Escuela Nueva programme   76, 127
Esenler Merkez   8–9, 127, 128
Etsy   175
e-Ranger   94
Europe   9, 12–13, 15–16, 32, 58, 69,
    90–1, 96, 122, 143, 150, 170
    companies   161
    economies   22
    leadership   159

F
Facebook   132, 134
First World War   94
Flynn, Tony   106
Fora do Eixo   131–2, 134
    Cube Card   133
    university   130
Ford, Henry   47, 60, 109

Ford Motor Company   66, 21
Fukusawa, Naoto   83, 153

G
Gansky, Lisa   130
Gates Foundation   55, 93, 146
General Electric (GE)   52, 83, 142,
    163, 179
    GE's Indian healthcare business   82
Germany   27, 160, 169
    Flensburg   171
    Freiburg   84, 99, 169–72, 180, 187
    Riesfeld   170
    Vauban   170
Ga, Ghana   72
Global Footprint Network   39
Google   133, 134
Goldman Sachs   10, 12, 108
Grameenphone's village phone   130
Greenlight Planet   100
Guatemala   76
Gulf States   69, 110
Gupta, Anil   52
    see also Honeybee Network
Gurgaon, India   14
    Belvedere   14
    Rockwood   14

H
Haiti   166
H&M   23
Harman   160–3
    see also Saras
Hart, Stuart   55–6
Harvard   2
Havana   116–17, 157, 182–3, 187
Hawkin, Paul   56
healthcare   2, 4, 20–1, 32, 49, 58, 63,
    77, 82, 90–1, 136, 143–5, 163–8
Heywood, Stephen   167
    see also Patients Like Me

HIV   99, 121–5, 136–7, 145, 156, 166–7
   see also AIDS
HMV   31
Hollywood   21
Honda   53
Honeybee Network   52
Hong Kong   11
Hoover   21
Houston   117
Hoy, Patrimonia   154
Hrudayala, Narayana   60
Husk Power Systems (HPS)   97–100, 145, 170, 188
Hyderabad, India   73

I
IDE   107
Ideal X   117–19
Ideo   48
India   1, 6, 10–16, 38–40, 51–3, 59–62, 72–3, 75, 77, 82–3, 86, 89–91, 96–9, 107, 110–12, 120, 128, 140, 145, 160, 162, 168, 170, 177–8, 187
   cities   13
   educational budget   75
   farmers   111
   healthcare business   82
   hospitals   77
   households   14
   schools   75
   society   14
Read India   89
Indonesia   11, 72, 75
   Jakarta   16
Inter American Development Bank   149
Internet   30, 35, 61, 132, 177, 179
   shopping   23
International Development Enterprises   55

International Finance Corporation (IFC)   99
Iran   110
Ireland   28, 84
Islam   41
Islamabad   40
Israel   108, 127, 145
Italy   17, 149

J
Japan   6, 31, 65, 85, 90–1, 149
   Japanese   60, 65–6
   producers   22
Jessops   31
Jobs, Steve   47–8
Jones, Daniel   67–8

K
Karachi   15–16, 72
Karnataka   59
Kaushik, Ravi   82
Kenya   1, 6, 94
   Bridge International Academy Network   73
Kenyan   64
Kerala   128–9, 166
Kickstarter   98, 107, 175
Kinshasa   16
Kiva   147
Kolkata   16
Kumar, Suresh   128–9, 135, 145, 156, 182, 187

L
Lagos   4, 16, 72
Lahore   15
Lambay, Farida   86, 88
Lawande, Sachin   160–2
Lean thinking   6, 63–5, 68, 77, 80, 97, 100, 103–4, 115, 118, 120, 138–9, 157, 182, 186

Lebanon   68, 158
  civil war   182
  Mount Lebanon   69
Lego   146
Lerner, Jaime   150
Librie   84
Life Straw, the   107
  see also Vestergaard Fransden
Lifespring   168
Lindblum, Charles   157
Linux   52
London   115–16
  Euston Station   19
  Guy's Hospital   59
Los Angeles   91
Lovins, Amory and Hunter   56

M
McDonald's   88, 145, 188
McKinsey Global Institute   37
McLean, Malcolm   117–20, 147
Maharashtra   87
Malaysia   115
Malawi   94, 166
Malmo   99, 172
Mandal, Mahila   88
Marks & Spencer   22
Massachusetts Institute of technology
      D-Lab   55
Medea, John   81
MedicallHome   62, 64, 77, 124, 156,
      165
Medicaid   167
Mercedes-Benz   12, 160
Medic Mobile   165–6
Merida   78
Mexico   11, 16, 63, 165, 188
  Campeche, Mexico   78
  Mexicans   1, 63, 64
  Mexico City   16, 62
MGM.com   175

Miami
  South Beach   11
  Vale   11
Midgley, Mary   43
Milburn, Joshua Field   30
MIT   81, 130
  MIT Media Lab   165
  Netra   165
Mitra, Sugata   75
Mobile Academy   166
Mother and Child Education Programme
      (Mocep)   76, 127–8, 136–7
Monash University   92–3, 143
  oxytocin aerosol   93, 184
Montblanc pen   12, 17
MOOCS   75
Mother Teresa   59
Mothers-2-Mothers (M2M)   123–6,
      136–7, 145, 156, 166, 188
Moreno, Israel   154
Morocco   100
M-Pesa   64–5, 77
Mtanga Dickson   166
Muji   83
Mumbai, India   16, 86–7, 89
  Municipal Corporation of   86–7
Munich   91, 108
Muscolevy, Rodrigo   148
Myanmar   11

N
Naandi   112, 143
Nagoya   65
Nairobi   16–17
  Kibera slum   16–17
  Mathare, North Nairobi   121, 123
Napster   177
Narita airport, Japan   18
Neighbourhood Network for Palliative
      Care (NNPC)   128–9, 137, 145,
      166

Netherlands, the   44, 84, 115
Nest   100
New Rin washing powder   12
New York   37, 55, 118, 150
NEWater Strategy   114
NH Group   60–2, 68–9, 168
NH Heart Hospitals   136, 143–5, 187
NHS   165
  Connecting for Health   165
Nicodemus, Ryan   30
Nigeria   11, 72, 75
  Lagos   16, 72
Noida, India   14
  Rockwood   14
Nokia   163
Norman, Donald   84
North Yorkshire   32
  Scarborough   32
Nuru Lights   100

O
OECD (Organisation for
    Economic Co-operation and
    Development)   15, 38, 42, 63
Office of Budget Responsibility   27
Ohno, Taiichi   66–7
Omega Chain   73
Omote Sando   11
  see also Toyota
O'Neil, Jim   10–12, 18
Osaka, Japan   110
Owen Falls Dam   40
  see also Uganda
Oxford University   86

P
PACT   167
  see also Behforouz, Louise
Pakistan   15, 40–1, 72, 73, 96
Citizens Foundation, Pakistan   73
Paliwal, Dinesh   160

Palo Alto   2
Pandey, Gyanesh   97, 100, 145, 182
Papanek, Victor   54
Partners in Health   166–7
  see also Prevention and Access to
    Care and Treatment
Patients Like Me   167
Paton, Charlie   108–10, 182
PEAS (Promoting Education in African
    Schools)   73
Pennsylvania   118
Pepsee   111, 120, 137
Peru   64, 72, 166
Pew Research   26
Phnom Penh   42, 99
Philippines   11
Piazzesi, Francesco   79
Polak, Paul   55, 82, 94
Polder Model   44
  see also the Netherlands
Poptech   48
Portland, Oregon   172
Prabhu, Jaideep   52
Prahalad, C. K.   55
Pratham   72, 86–90, 99, 125, 143,
    147, 156–7, 188
  see also India
Prevention and Access to Care and
    Treatment   166
  see also Partners in health
Pro-Am movement   174
Procter & Gamble   163
Prototyping   152
PRS-500   84–5
Pune   86
Punjab   15

R
Radjou, Navi   52
R & D Labs   47, 58, 118
Rane, Usha   86

Raspberry Pi   172–4, 178
  foundation   173
Reagan, Ronald   21
Renault-Nissan   179
recession   3, 9, 11, 31
  great recession   25, 27–9
Resolution Foundation, the   27
Ries, Eric   156
River Rouge Plant   66
Rosling, Hans   36, 45
Russia   10
Rwanda   73, 100

S

Sabis group   68–71, 74, 77, 158, 182
  schools   70, 127
Safeway supermarket   20
Sagir, Aziz   8, 10, 76, 127
Samsung   163
Sanders, Doug   17
Santa Clara University's frugal design
  lab   54
São Paulo   9, 16, 131–3, 150
Saras   160–2
  see also Harman
Sarvajal   112–13, 188
Saumweber, Philip   108–9
Schumacher, E. F.   53–4, 56–7, 60
Schwarz Michael   57
Seattle   118
Seawater Greenhouse   108
Second World War   20, 24, 65, 98,
  107, 118
Senge, Peter   44
Shakti, Grammen   100
Shanzai companies   52
Shetty, Devy   59–62, 144
Singapore   113–15, 117, 158, 182, 187
Silicon Valley   23, 59
Skype   61

Slim, Carlos   64
Smith, Adam   135
Smith, Amy   55
SMS   83
Sony   84–5
South Africa   121–2, 145
Soviet Union   116, 183
Spain   28
Spectrum ZX   172
Square   175
Stanford's Programme of
    Entrepreneurial Design for
    Extreme Environments   54
STERN Review of Climate Change   38
Stevens, Dominic   84
Student Life organisation   74
Sundrop Farm   108, 110
Suzuki   53

T

Taniguchi, Cassio   150
Tantlinger, Keith   118–20, 147
Tanzania   92
Tata Ace   82, 85
Tata Swach   107–8, 112, 142
TED   48
Tesco   23
Texas   37
Thatcher, Margaret   21
Thingiverse   52, 175
Threadless   175
Toyoda, Kiichiro   66
  see also Toyota
Toyota   6, 59, 65–8, 74, 77, 79, 100,
    157, 182
  Toyota Landcruiser   94
  Toyota production system   68–70
  see also Sabis group
Tuas desalination plant   114
Tunisia   110

Turkey   11, 76, 127–8, 145
    Istanbul   4, 9
        Turkish dolmus   18
Trade Unions   21
Travelodge   82
Twitter   83, 134

U
Udacity   75
Uganda   40, 73
    Lake Victoria   40
UK   20, 21–2, 27–8, 31–2, 59, 69–70,
    145, 165, 173, 177–8
UK Economy   10, 22
UK Supermarkets   22
UN Millennium Ecosystems
    Assessment 39
UNICEF   86
Unilever   163, 179
Upton, Eben   173–4
    see also Raspberry Pi
US   9–12, 15–16, 20–2, 26–8, 30,
    37–9, 58, 60–1, 66–7, 69, 91,
    96–7, 106, 116–18, 121–2, 143,
    145, 161, 167, 171, 175
    US companies   22
    US Navy   107

V
Valencia, Spain   168

Varga, Vasantik   87
Vasool, Paisa   13–14, 30, 49
Vestergaard Fransden   107
    see also The Life Straw
Vietnam   11, 42
Virgin Pendolino train   19

W
Walmart   23, 59, 145
Wall Street   24
Water   1–4, 12–13, 15, 17–18, 35–7,
    39–44, 65, 78–9, 91, 96, 101,
    103–17, 120, 132, 142–3, 158–9,
    176, 182–3, 185, 187–8
Whole Earth catalogue   132
Wikipedia   52, 130
Wired magazine   48, 174
Womak, James   67–8
Wonga   31
World Bank   72, 106
World Economic Forum   12

Y
Yamaha   53
Yrigoyen, Pedro   62–3, 64
YouTube   134

Z
Zara   23
Zipcar   130

Printed and bound by CPI Group (UK) Ltd, Croydon, CR0 4YY